OUR BLITZ

RED SKIES OVER MANCHESTER

A WARTIME FACSIMILE

AURORA PUBLISHING

This edition published by:
AURORA PUBLISHING
Unit 9, Bradley Fold Trading Estate,
Radcliffe Moor Road, Bradley Fold,
Bolton, BL2 6RT.
Tel: 0204 370752
Fax: 0204 370751

Originally published in 1945
by Kemsley Newspapers Limited

Cover photograph:
Fighting the flames in Manchester.

ISBN 1 85926 049 7

Printed by:
Manchester Free Press,
Longford Trading Estate,
Thomas Street, Stretford,
Manchester M32 0JT.

Thanks to Cliff Hayes, for his discovery
of the original material for this title,
and to Bob Bonner, of the Manchester Fire
Service, for additional photographs supplied.

INTRODUCTION

A T THIS TIME of anniversaries – the recent 50th anniversary of D-Day and the 50th anniversary of Victory in Europe Day – it seemed appropriate to reprint this wartime booklet about the bombing attacks suffered in the Manchester area. Anyone who did not experience the Blitz will be able to see for themselves what it meant, and what the people of Manchester suffered during World War II (1939-45).

This reprint not only records faithfully the high and low points of the City's commitment and punishment, but also offers a collection of the feelings of different writers, feelings of pride, relief, sadness and anger – but never defeat!

The War years are shown through the eyes of newspaper reports. These should be of particular interest to young people, who may make comparisons with modern-day war coverage and who will be surprised at the devastation inflicted upon Manchester, alongside many other British cities. It will also bring back mixed memories to those who lived in Manchester during the War years.

It was tempting to alter some of the captions – for example, to point out that the picture on page 17, of the bombed-out Shambles Square is now the area at the back door of Marks & Spencer, but a little imagination will help people to place most of the pictures. Due to Wartime censorship – in an attempt to keep up morale, and not publicise too much War activity – this booklet, produced in 1945 was the first time many Mancunians had seen these pictures or read the stories.

Reading through this book makes us realise how lucky we are, and how much is owed to the brave men and women, many of whom died, were maimed or permanently injured throughout World War II, to realise just a little of what they suffered and to hope and pray that such devastation never happens again!

CITY PEOPLE

UNBREAKABLE!—HOMELESS CHRISTMAS MORNING, 1940

OUR BLITZ

The Daily Dispatch

AND

Evening Chronicle

record in Story and Picture of
the German Bombing Attacks
on the Greater Manchester area,
with special reference to the
nights December **22 & 23**, 1940

Red Sky Over Manchester

Foreword by

THE EARL OF DERBY, K.G.

The whole of the proceeds from the sale of "OUR BLITZ" will be
given to "The Daily Dispatch" and "Evening Chronicle" War Fund

PRICE 2s. 6d.

PRINTED AND PUBLISHED BY

KEMSLEY NEWSPAPERS LIMITED

KEMSLEY HOUSE   MANCHESTER 4

FOREWORD

BY

THE EARL OF DERBY, K.G.

NO finer example of the moral strength of a nation is to be found in history than in the resistance of the British people to the mass raids of the Luftwaffe in 1940 and 1941. In that resistance Manchester and its neighbouring towns played a tremendous part.

The patient and uncomplaining endurance by the people of our country of unparalleled dangers and hardships has contributed as surely to the victory which is now within our grasp as the heroism of our armies on many battle fronts.

If they had failed all would have been lost. But they did not fail, and in fighting with such matchless courage as they did through long and weary months of terror from the air, they wrote a page of Northern history which will stir the hearts and minds of men and women in the years to come.

In the toll of precious lives, in the ruins of many famous buildings in Manchester and surrounding districts, in the shattered factories and business houses whose products and enterprises were known all over the world, in the devastated houses of many thousands of good citizens, one sees the price which has been paid for freedom.

It was a heavy price, paid in suffering and grief and sadness, yet with spiritual exaltation, too, for there was no man, nor any woman, who did not sense the greatness of the hour and the crisis which lay upon our beloved country.

I write this foreword in humble dedication to the gallant men and women of the blitzed areas of Greater Manchester who gave their lives in service to their fellow-men, and to the people whose serene spirit and calm courage brought them triumphantly through the ordeal of nights made hideous by bomb and fire.

It is my hope that out of the old scarred Manchester a new city will arise, animated by new concepts of a fuller life, revivified by civic pride and mutual helpfulness so nobly born, and inspired always by the story told so vividly in this book.

THE PLAN BEHIND CIVIL DEFENCE

By HARTLEY SHAWCROSS
(North-West Regional Commissioner)

ON THE 8th AUGUST, 1940, in the first air attack on the Manchester area, the enemy dropped with a few high-explosive and incendiary bombs a missile of a different kind. It was a bundle of leaflets labelled, for some reason not made apparent by the contents, " Hitler's last appeal to reason." It had failed to open in the air and, unreasonably enough, it fell upon the head of a police officer guarding the entrance to the Civil Defence Report and Control Centre in Salford.

But Hitler's actions had appealed to the citizens of south-east Lancashire more clearly than his leaflets were likely to do—and very much earlier. For, although in the peaceful days of 1937 and 1938 wishful thinking led most of us to hope that the enemy's bombers would never be heard over England, and least of all over Manchester, there were large numbers of public-spirited citizens who understood the lessons of Austria, of Albania, of Munich; who saw the dangers ahead and who, under the Air Raid Precautions Act of 1937, prepared for them by building up the framework of a Civil Defence machine or by enrolling in one or other of the services which were established.

Sometimes we watched them, curiously, at their exercises; sometimes we smiled, tolerantly and condescendingly, at the way in which they gave up their Sundays and their evenings to training. But they submitted to our curiosity, bore with our smiles and condescension—and carried on with their work.

And so, when war came, south-east Lancashire, as the rest of the country, was not entirely unprepared. Already in the various Civil Defence Services there were considerable numbers of part-time personnel; men and women, of an astonishing diversity of class, age and occupation, who had devoted their peaceful summer evenings to training against the then-unbelievable horrors of war: already there was a machine, although not so comprehensive or elaborate as it later became, for controlling and directing the operations of Civil Defence; already the local authorities had established Emergency Committees with full powers capable of dealing expeditiously with any situation which might arise. With war the full machinery of wartime Civil Defence was brought into operation.

Recruits Pour In

The organisation of the Regional Commissioners, set up to co-ordinate the work of Government departments and local authorities and, if necessary, to take over full control in case of emergency, which existed in skeleton form, came into force. The Controllers, generally the Clerks of the County Councils and County Boroughs or the Chief Constables, in charge of Civil Defence arrangements consulted with the Emergency Committees of their Councils and with the heads of the various Services, and manned their Report and Control Centres ready for action. Large numbers of part-time personnel volunteered for whole-time duty, and many thousands of recruits came into the different services.

Throughout south-east Lancashire on the 3rd September, 1939, the Civil Defence Services were at their action posts, ready for the attack which they were warned might come. It did not come. One long peaceful night succeeded another. Poland seemed, perhaps, a long way away— surely, such things couldn't happen to us. The bombing of Warsaw was not the bombing of Wythenshawe. And, as time went on, there were not a few who began again to think that the bombers never would come to Manchester : that, somehow or other, a solution would be found.

But not so in Civil Defence. It was a time of intensive training ; the size of the Services was being vastly increased ; problems of organisation and equipment which had not previously been recognised were being dealt with ; new Services were being developed. And so throughout the winter of 1939 and the early spring of 1940. Then came the German offensive in the West—Rotterdam— that was uncomfortably nearer ! There was an air service between Ringway and—was it ?—Rotterdam before the war. Preparations against air attack gained added impetus. Still more men and women put aside personal convenience and comfort in order to join the services. But still no attack came.

The First Warning

Then at last, in the midsummer of 1940, at fourteen minutes past three in the morning of the 20th June, there came, on the teleprinter and the telephone lines, that terse, sombre message : " Air raid warning Red " ; for the first time the wailing note of the siren rose and fell in earnest. And it was taken in earnest, that first warning. Civilians went to their shelters ; Civil Defence personnel were everywhere on their toes ; Controllers and Sub-Controllers hurried to their posts. At their Report and Control Centres telephones were manned, members of the services sat with their message report forms at their allotted places round the table, ready to deal with reports as they came in from the Wardens Posts, from the Police, from the Fire Brigades, and to send out the necessary assistance.

But although the full-throated drone of enemy aircraft was heard there were no bombs, no guns, no " incidents." But south-east Lancashire knew now that " they " could get here : perhaps it had been a reconnaissance—fore-runner of things to come. Five weeks went by and nothing came.

Then, on the 29th July a stray aeroplane dropped a bomb in the Salford area. There was no prior warning that night, but, fortunately, no casualties were caused, and damage was slight. Thereafter the sirens sounded more often but bombs were infrequent, and in the City of Manchester itself it was not until the 28-29th August that the first bombs fell, a stick being dropped in the Brooklands road district, causing, however, comparatively little damage.

As the number of small, scattered raids increased, the

THESE
WERE
THEIR
HOMES

Civil Defence organisation worked, on the whole, smoothly and efficiently, gradually adapting and improving its arrangements to meet the problems disclosed by actual experience of attack. Sometimes individual members of the services failed to act in accordance with the prescribed procedure, and temporary confusion resulted : sometimes, on the other hand, an unauthorised departure from routine showed how the procedure could be improved.

And thus the Manchester area was gradually broken in to enemy raids, learning a little from each one as it occurred, but still not being subjected to any concentration of attack. By December, 1940, however, the Civil Defence plans against such an attack had been largely reviewed and completed. In Manchester itself the Town Clerk was the Controller in charge of the City's Civil Defence Services, and at the same time was the Group Officer for Mutual Support for what is known as the South-East Lancashire Group, comprising that constellation of important industrial towns of which Manchester is the centre.

This group organisation formed a vital part of the machinery of Civil Defence. It was set up partly to facilitate the movement of reinforcements, the Group Officer having the sole authority, under the Regional Commissioner, to call for parties to be sent from one town to another in the group as the need arose, and partly to decentralise the control exercised by the Regional Commissioner during air raid conditions, the Group Officer constituting a link between the various local authorities in the group and the Regional War Room.

It was an organisation which was soon to prove its value in south-east Lancashire, as it had already on Merseyside. But until it had been proved there were still some local authorities anxious, and very properly so, to know how their machine would operate if subjected to severe attacks such as Sheffield, Coventry and Birmingham had experienced. Indeed, about the middle of December discussions arose as to whether it would be desirable for members of an Emergency Committee to visit one of the towns in another region which had been heavily attacked in order to see for themselves the problems which had arisen, and how they had been dealt with.

But the question—not easy to answer, for there were substantial reasons against such visits at that time—was automatically disposed of. The letter on which the matter was raised with the Regional Commissioner is endorsed : " This was settled by the Manchester Blitz : put away."

And when, on that fateful Sunday evening, December 22nd, the sirens heralded the commencement of the Luftwaffe's most furious onslaught, the task of the Group Officers for Mutual Support was not an easy one, for it was not immediately clear where the main enemy attack was to fall, and a movement of reinforcements towards Manchester might have left the Liverpool area insufficiently protected. Liverpool had already been severely raided on the 20th and 21st, and, indeed, throughout the night of the 22nd-23rd bombs did fall in the Merseyside area. But it was not long before Region were able to form a reasonably

THE IMPRESSIVE LINES OF THE DOME OF VICTORIA BUILDINGS WERE REVEALED FOR THE FIRST TIME BY THE COLLAPSE OF SURROUNDING WALLS, BUT THE DOME ITSELF SOON DISAPPEARED AS THE WHOLE BLOCK HAD TO BE DEMOLISHED AS UNSAFE

exact appreciation, and to direct available reinforcements into the Manchester area.

Next night the enemy came again. The raid was a shorter one, but the cumulative effect of the two raids was severe. The main problem had been fire. In all there were 1,300 fires in Manchester and the surrounding areas. At that time the Fire Services had not been nationalised, and although the local brigades, greatly augmented as they were by the Auxiliary Fire Service, did valiant and admirable work, the situation was far beyond local resources.

As in the Civil Defence general services, so with the fire brigades there were local area schemes for reinforcement. These were brought into operation, but the position was complicated by the fact that three local authority areas, Manchester, Salford, and Stretford, were under attack, and although brigades moved in from all over Lancashire and Cheshire they alone were not enough.

All the brigades worked splendidly, and in time a very big force was built up. In all, some 400 additional appliances were brought in and over 3,400 additional men —but the lack of a common command and organisation and also of standardised methods and equipment was a serious handicap, and there was no adequate directional staff to control the large numbers of men who came in from so many different areas.

When the second night's attack began the greater part of the personnel were completely fatigued, yet they fought the fresh fires with great vigour and determination. Yet although thousands of firemen worked all day on the 23rd, throughout the night, and again through the following day, fires were still showing a glare on the night of Christmas Eve, and it was not until the afternoon of Christmas Day that the Regional Commissioner was able to report to the Government that the fire situation throughout the area was under control; even then it was not until some time later that all fires were extinguished.

As in the case of the fire brigades, so with the other Civil Defence Services; the situation was sometimes beyond the capacity of the local personnel alone. They had to take the first shock of the attack, and they took it with great courage and efficiency. Members of the Manchester Rescue Service had already had two very hard nights on Merseyside, but, tired as they were, they turned out again.

Rapidly the Group Controller called in reinforcements from other areas in the group, and Regional Control brought in parties from elsewhere. By the morning of December 23rd ninety whole-time Rescue Parties were on duty in Manchester alone, apart from the part-time members of the service.

The Wardens Service, working always in conditions of great danger, functioned admirably. They were the eyes and ears of Civil Defence, and they never failed.

The Casualty Services—hospitals, First Aid Posts, First Aid Parties, and ambulance workers—too, carried out their grim duties gallantly, although in Manchester four out of ten hospitals were put completely out of action. When a mobile First Aid Post was hit, and some of the staff, including the Medical Officer, were killed, those of the personnel who escaped injury were immediately reformed into fresh teams, and carried on with their duties.

AT THE CITY CENTRE

EXPLOSIVE AND INCENDIARY BOMBS COMBINED TO PRODUCE THIS SCENE OF DEVASTATION IN THE CANNON STREET AREA

On one journey a young ambulance attendant, a peacetime waitress, arrived at an incident where a woman in labour had just been rescued from her damaged home. On the way to the hospital the baby was born, the attendant having the ambulance pulled up in a side street and calmly undertaking the rôle of a midwife.

So also with the Police. Reinforcements were brought in under pre-arranged schemes, and although a heavy strain was thrown upon them, it speaks highly, both for their efficiency and tact and for the high morale of the civilian population, that never once did any anxiety arise in regard to the maintenance of law and order.

One more body of workers must be praised for their sterling service, the women volunteers in the Rest Centre Service of the W.V.S.—splendid women whose help never failed.

Rapid Restoration

Despite the efficiency of all these services, however, damage and dislocation was serious. On the 23rd, on the 24th, and again on Christmas Day the Regional Commissioner held conferences of high officials of Government departments, of local authorities, and of services concerned. At these " post-blitz " conferences, as they were called, the whole situation was reviewed, demands for assistance were co-ordinated and supplied and measures were initiated to restore the general life and industry of the area.

By Christmas Day the Regional Commissioner was able to report to the Government that the work of restoration was " going on rapidly : Services have worked magnificently. Local authorities are functioning admirably, and there is highest co-operation in all directions . . . the spirit of the people remains excellent, and Manchester has been able to celebrate its Christmas." By December 27th people were streaming to work in Manchester as normally as the traffic situation, still not fully restored, would allow, and by the beginning of January it was possible to say that Manchester's contribution to the war effort would not be seriously reduced.

By that time, also, the assistance of the military in such matters as debris clearance and traffic control had been largely dispensed with. The Emergency Committee of the Manchester City Council asked the Regional Commissioner to thank the military authorities for their assistance, and it is worthy of record that in his reply General Gordon Finlayson, the Army Commander, said :

I have read with great interest the report of the Emergency Committee. It impresses one with the immense amount of organising work put in by the Civil and Regional authorities, and makes one realise how little there would be of Manchester if it had not been for that foresight and work.

As an example of the effect of that work, the small number of soldiers asked for was a triumph in itself, proving the worth of the Civil preparations.

But that high praise was not earned without cost in life and limb. By the time the last raid in August, 1942, was over, sixty-four men and women in the Police, Fire and Civil Defence services in the Manchester area had paid with their lives, and about 250 had been injured.

All this was two years ago. Since then the Civil Defence Services have been standing by ; waiting lest the enemy dare to come again. There have been changes and alterations. Large numbers of whole-time personnel have

"——REMOVED TO."—BOMBED-OUT BUSINESS MEN MOVING OFFICE FURNITURE TO HURRIEDLY-FOUND EMERGENCY PREMISES

been released for service in the Forces or in industry. The Fire Service has been nationalised. Mobile Columns, under the control of the Regional Commissioner, have largely replaced the whole-time Rescue personnel employed by the local authorities. More and more the Services depend on the efficient and enthusiastic work of part-time personnel.

Just as in the autumn of 1939 there were those who scoffed or said the enemy would never come, so now there are those who profess to think he will not come again. But the Civil Defence personnel, now supported in many cases by the most valuable assistance of the Home Guard, carry on. They do not underestimate the force which the enemy can still direct against us ; they know the danger of a desperate foe at bay : they realise the grave consequences which might follow if this great centre of production were to be caught unprepared. And they are determined to remain prepared, and to maintain the high tradition which they have built up.

It is dull, irksome work ; work lacking the glamour and the praise of those days years ago when the fate of England depended in large measure upon our Civil Defence personnel. But it is work as vital still to-day if our insurance against enemy attack from the air is to be maintained till the risk is over. That time may, we hope, come soon : it is not yet. Until it comes the Civil Defence Services will stand to their posts, knowing that in total war victory will come only by the united effort of a united people.

There, in broad outline, is the Civil Defence plan set up by Government and local authorities in case of war : how it stood up to the impact of the real thing you will be able to judge for yourselves as the details are filled in by the other contributors to this volume.

COMMUNICATIONS: CITY
RAILWAYMEN'S COURAGE
DEFEATS THE LUFTWAFFE

MORE THAN ONCE THROUGHOUT THE SERIES OF RAIDS THE RAILWAYS
WERE HIT, BUT NEVER SO BADLY THAT THE RESOURCEFULNESS—AND
OFTEN GREAT COURAGE—OF THE TRANSPORT WORKERS COULD NOT
OVERCOME THE DIFFICULTIES IN INCREDIBLY SHORT TIME. ON OPPOSITE
PAGE IS A PICTURE OF THE HAVOC AT A CITY GOODS YARD, WHILE ABOVE IS
THE RESULT OF THE REMARKABLE " SNOWBALL " COLLAPSE OF THE OLD
VIADUCT CARRYING THE ALTRINCHAM ELECTRIC LINE. ONE ARCH WAS
PIERCED BY A BOMB ; DURING REPAIR WORK THE ARCH COLLAPSED,
THEN ARCH AFTER ARCH FOLLOWED, BURYING SEVERAL WORKMEN

THE GREAT ATTACK FAILS

By WILLIAM MULLIGAN AND RICHARD WALKER

Manchester was the target last night of strong German bomber formations. According to reports so far received, important factories were destroyed by heavy hits, and extensive fires and many violent explosions caused.
Official German News Agency, December 23, 1940.

Last night strong formations of German bombers again attacked Manchester and London. Several large and numerous small fires were caused in London, and especially in Manchester.
German Communiqué, December 24, 1940.

MANY WEEKS BEFORE the assault of the Luftwaffe on the Greater Manchester area on the nights of December 22-23 and December 23-24, 1940, the residents had cast away the fond and heartwarming illusion that enemy raiders could not cross the Pennines in any strength, and that the everlasting pall of smoke would blot out the city from aerial observation.

The mood of tense expectancy thus created - was heightened when, on the two preceding nights, December 20-21 and 21-22, Merseyside was heavily raided, and citizens of Manchester, Salford, Stretford and neighbouring towns spent more than fifteen hours at their posts of duty or in the shelters.

After these two nights it was inconceivable that Manchester could escape. Its importance in the war effort was not less than that of Sheffield ; it ran Liverpool very close as a strategic centre : its great industries, its position in the chain of distribution, its teeming population together constituted a target not likely to be overlooked by the war lords of the Nazi machine.

At 6-38 in the evening of December 22 the sirens flung their warning on the cold night air, penetrating into the cosy Sunday home-life of many thousands of residents, calling out the members of the defence services to their posts, warning the mercifully few who were in the city that night that they must seek shelter.

It was Manchester's moment of destiny, as it was Salford's and Stretford's, and that of many other smaller townships and villages. From that moment began the greatest ordeal in the area's history ; an ordeal which was to cost the lives of many hundreds of citizens, which destroyed or damaged thousands of homes and business premises, which spread suffering, hardship and sorrow throughout the district so that few were untouched by the consequences, and none failed to gather experiences which will endure in the memory till their dying day.

The Nazi sword of terror was double-edged. By one gigantic stroke it was to destroy and paralyse the war potential of the area ; by another it was to wreak upon public morale such fear of the might of the German Reich that the people would urge upon their leaders the futility of fighting on, and the necessity to sue for peace. This was the strategic picture painted in blood and flame by the organisers of the German plan to eliminate their last enemy, city by city and town by town. Their trump card was panic, and it was defeated by the fortitude and high courage of the people of the area.

By these qualities material damage and injury were made to appear as puny, insignificant things against the spiritual force of united resistance and endurance. The reactions of the ordinary citizen were characteristic and simple. His anger, grudgingly expressed, was mingled with disgust that women and children should be thus brutally brought into the front line. He wanted more than anything else to keep the wheels of industry moving so that we should not lack the material with which to hit back. He was filled with quiet pride in himself and his fellow-men and women. The ordeal had come and was over. He knew he had it in him to take what still remained for him to take. There were few people who did not feel the same emotions.

Remembering these things, it is in pride but not vainglory, in humility but not self-depreciation, we tell the story of the two nights of the blitz, with many details which have not been revealed before, and many pictures which for reasons of security could not be released until now.

And in doing so, it should be said that militarily and administratively the attack, though it covered two nights, is regarded as one indivisible raid, and all records of the assault are based upon this proposition.

Grim though their ordeal was, few of the hundreds of thousands who were in Manchester and the surrounding areas throughout the two-night blitz had anything like a comprehensive picture of the battle which raged about them. They knew little of the titanic struggle being played out behind the scenes to meet the terrific blows of the enemy, to thwart his strategy, to keep industry going, to maintain those essential services which had become enemy targets, and to lesson the force of the impact on the citizens at large, and the victims in particular.

Learning—For The Future

The compiling of the first official comprehensive picture was begun by the Manchester Emergency Committee a few days after the blitz—even while hundreds of Civil Defence workers were battling with the aftermath. But that story remained an official secret, except to a limited few whose duty it was to count the cost—and to learn the lessons for what might yet be to come.

Many weeks passed, however, before all the pieces of the grim jig-saw could be fitted together. By that time, Manchester, Salford, Stretford and their scarred neighbours were too engrossed in their war labours, their personal affairs, their major problems and their minor interests to concern themselves with much more than had revealed itself to them in the seared landscape from which familiar landmarks had now vanished. War is impatient in its headlong stride.

The sirens were already a familiar sound when they wailed again on the night of Sunday, December 22. Most people had barely finished their evening meal ; black-out restrictions had already established mid-afternoon Evensong services in the churches, and the day's religious devotions had prematurely closed.

GUTTED WAREHOUSES IN MILLER STREET, WHERE BLOCK AFTER BLOCK OF THE GREAT GROUP OF WAREHOUSES OWNED BY BAXENDALE'S, LTD., WAS DESTROYED

The twelve hours which followed were Manchester's time of testing

The raid followed the plan adopted by the enemy in their massed assaults on other cities. There was a preliminary intensive incendiary attack, during which few high-explosive bombs were used, followed by the bombardment by increasingly-heavy calibre high-explosive bombs as the target area became illuminated by the fires caused by the showers of incendiaries.

The first incendiaries were showered over the city two minutes after the alarm was sounded, and the fire-fighting services were in action from that time onwards at a *tempo* which mounted almost to breaking point—sustained there only by human will and determination which triumphed over failing human energergies.

One of the first incendiary bombs dropped in the central city area of Manchester fell in Albert Square, opposite the Princess Street corner of the Town Hall. In a few minutes the building on the corner of Princess Street and Clarence Street was ablaze—one of the first of the city's casualties.

Two minutes later an incendiary was reported from the corner of Bridgewater Street and Chepstow Street. It had struck the door of an air raid shelter. Incendiaries were reported to have set the top of the Royal Exchange ablaze; Victoria Buildings were alight, the gas main in Hailwood's Creamery in St. Mary's Gate was gushing fire, and in a few minutes part of Victoria Buildings had collapsed into Deansgate, blocking the thoroughfare from Blackfriars Street to Victoria Bridge, with the overhead wires of the tramway system tangled up beneath the piles of debris.

The flood of reports of " incidents " had begun to pour in to Main Control. In those first few minutes wardens had extinguished an incendiary in the Cathedral Yard; Exchange Hotel was blazing fiercely; Burton's tailor's shop at the corner of Corporation Street and Market Street was on fire; wardens and firemen were frantically smothering a fire which threatened to engulf Bridgewater House, that massive pile behind the Palace Theatre, and more incendiaries were having their vicious life smothered out of them on the roof of the C.P.A. buildings.

The airborne incendiary had broken loose. From the skies he applied his blazing brand first to one building and then another; then to groups of buildings, to rows of humble cottages, to the dwellings in the outer fringe of the city, and to the villas in the suburbs.

Within the hour, warehouses at the corner of Portland Street and Sackville Street, in Watson Street and elsewhere were in the grip of fire and already doomed to destruction, blocking the roads over which they had cast their shadow through generations of peaceful commerce and trading.

Communications between Manchester and Salford by way of Bridge Street had been severed by the collapse of a building at the corner of Bridge Street and Gartside Street. Self-appointed " wardens " had joined forces with the official Civil Defence workers and police in battling against showers of incendiaries which had cascaded down on to the children's recreation grounds of George's Park, Hulme, and in the surrounding streets—Erskine Street, Russell Street and Lime Street; high explosives were blasting buildings asunder or falling impotently on open ground, to bite craters in the earth and leave their ugly marks as objects of curiosity when daylight came.

Three high explosives fell among a shower of incendiaries in St. George's Park. One of them scored a direct hit on an underground shelter which, happily, was unoccupied; another dropped in the children's paddling pool; the third fell harmlessly on open ground.

In the Oxford Road area many homes were damaged in the vicinity of Gray Street, Stafford Street and Cooke Street. From these homes 341 people were driven to seek temporary shelter at Wood Street Mission.

All the time the Civil Defence services carried on with the tasks for which they had trained laboriously, patiently and ungrudgingly throughout the preceding months. The official records bear testimony to their selfless service. In the bulging dossiers of messages and reports preserved in the archives of the Civil Defence you will still find, with almost monotonous recurrence, such messages as this:

Rescue party returned to "X" depot back from Blank Street. Fit for further service.

Nothing in those simple words of the struggle to rescue victims from death which threatened them amid the ruins of what had been their homes or their works; nothing of how the rescuers had flirted with death itself in their work of succour; nothing of the overpowering fatigue of their labours. They had completed their task at one "incident." They were "fit for further service."

One typical "incident" was that at the corner of Great Jackson Street and City Road, where a H.E. had dropped, killing one man and causing havoc to surrounding property. The foreman of the rescue squad reported in due course that even if the debris were removed the street would continue to be unsafe to traffic owing to the dangerous condition of the overshadowing buildings. He asked simply if he could take his squad "to any incident more important."

That was the spirit which actuated them. Personal safety was forgotten; their one concern was where the greater need lay.

450 Trapped—All Saved

Greater Manchester was lucky in at least one respect. Though there were lives lost when shelters received direct hits or the full blast of H.E.'s, not one major tragedy occurred in any of the shelters. There were many alarming moments; many more alarmist rumours. For example, 450 people were trapped during the first of the blitz raids in what was known as Gibson's shelter in Erskine Street, Stretford Road, which officially was intended to accommodate only 200. But every one was rescued alive.

There were rumours that a catastrophe had occurred in a shelter at Cornbrook. It was, happily, just rumour, though four people lost their lives there. And if any placed credence in those rumours it is not unfitting, even at this late hour, to dispel them as just rumour.

Rumour was not entirely without its humours. There was the occasion, four days after the first heavy raid, when much consternation was caused by the discovery of what were believed to be unexploded bombs under some premises in Market Street. The official services were hastened into action, to discover that they were nothing worse than dummy bombs which had been used for an exhibition.

But that did not solve the worry. Passers-by did not know they were only dummies, and they caused the police much trouble by continually reporting the presence of "U.E.B.'s"—unexploded bombs—until a smart warden

hit on a simple idea. If he could be instructed to place a cover over the bombs and obscure them from the view he thought it would "meet the situation." He was "instructed." And it did.

That, by the way. Four days after the blitz was a more fitting time for humour than when fire and destruction were raining down out of the night, when the earth trembled and shook with the blast of bombs and the roar of A.A. batteries which played with a distant and fearful enchantment against the black curtain of the night.

On the first night of the blitz at least 233 H.E. bombs were rained on Manchester alone. No accurate record of the number of incendiaries which were released over the area is possible, but the number ran into many thousands.

On the second night, during which the attack lasted from 7-15 p.m. on Monday until 1-29 a.m. on Tuesday, thousands of incendiary bombs were again dropped, and at least 55 H.E.'s left their toll of death and destruction.

By three o'clock on the afternoon of January 2, 1941, Manchester authorities knew the toll of the blitz in life and limb. The dead in Manchester numbered 363; there were 455 seriously injured hospital cases; 728 more people had been treated for less serious wounds.

They Lessened The Toll

But for the selfless service of the various branches of the Civil Defence, the police and the fire forces the toll would have been much heavier. Rescue parties, for instance, were turned out to 501 incidents. They rescued 226 people alive; it was their task to recover from the ruins and desolation no fewer than 256 bodies.

The wardens, too, played their heroic part. The number of messages they transmitted by every means at their command, bringing into play the intricate and comprehensive range of services to cope with the ever-changing situations, ran into thousands. Enormous files—dozens, hundreds of them, tucked away in the archives of the various A.R.P. authorities—bear testimony to the efficiency with which they carried out their duties.

The fire services faced a task which up to that time—the Liverpool and London fire raids came later—was without precedent in the staggering demands made not only upon its personnel, but its equipment. Some of their gallant members paid with their lives; others were maimed in the cause of duty.

In Manchester alone there were six officially-designated "conflagrations," 20 major fires, and 600—this, the authorities acknowledge, was only a modest estimate—serious, medium, small and minor fires.

Manchester had 200 of its firefighters and 30 of its pumps in Liverpool helping to quell the fire and fury of the raids on Merseyside when the blitz switched over to Manchester. Within two minutes of the alarm being sounded the city's fire services were called into action.

With an ever-rising insistence the call for firefighters poured in from every quarter of the city. Within one and a half hours the whole of the available mobile fire units, down to the old-fashioned hand escapes which had been cast aside for more modern equipment, were in action. Manchester was not alone in its demands. Fires were raging in Salford and in Stretford on a scale which demanded every ounce of local resources. Calls were sent outside the area for assistance. At 8-15 p.m. the first of the outside units entered into the fight. It came from Hazel Grove.

UNTOUCHED BY TIME—AND WAR. WITH COMPARATIVELY MODERN BUILDINGS ALL ROUND IT DESTROYED OR BADLY DAMAGED, YE OLDE WELLINGTON INN, AT THE CORNER OF MARKET PLACE AND THE SHAMBLES, WAS STILL STANDING AFTER MANCHESTER'S HEAVIEST RAID. IT WAS BUILT IN THE FIFTEENTH CENTURY.

While the skies glowed with the reflection from the countless fires another disaster seriously impeded the firefighters. The Godley water main was smashed by enemy action, and the firemen were forced back on the severely-taxed resources of the static water supplies.

The firemen battled through the night against raging fires, while bombs rained down on them from the skies, and empty shells of burned-out buildings threatened to collapse and destroy them. When the workers of Manchester began to flock into the city in the morning, firemen were playing their hoses on the roof of the Royal Exchange, where the flames still flickered persistently. It was already obvious that serious damage had been wrought, but how serious was not to be known for another twenty-four hours. Then it was found that high explosives of heavy calibre which had struck the massive building within the first few minutes of the raid had destroyed nearly half the floor space of the Exchange itself, and the subsequent fire had consumed the quarters of merchants and familiar shopping premises which were housed in the building.

Undaunted, the Royal Exchange carried on. For several days members held their " market " in the nearby streets until accommodation was arranged at the Houldsworth Hall, where business was conducted until temporary repairs enabled the members to return to their old home, sixteen weeks after the Luftwaffe had struck their blow.

To-day the Royal Exchange still bears many signs of the battering it received—but, in keeping with the spirit of Manchester, " carries on " as though nothing had happened.

By 11-30 on the morning of December 23 every fire in the city was under control. The firemen were still pouring water on to the burning debris that night when the Luftwaffe returned to the attack. Though fatigued, they faced up to the task with a spirit and vigour which

amazed even their own officers. Once again the first waves of raiders poured thousands of incendiaries over the area, and subsequent waves dropped their high explosives into the midst of the fires. Once more deadly peril menaced the fire-fighters. But they carried on.

In many cases they had to return to the scene of the previous night's battles to recover equipment which lay buried beneath the debris and pumps which were " standing by " before they could go into battle again. The previous night's grim experiences were not without their lessons. Fire-fighting units, including those which came in from outside districts, instead of being housed in the fire brigade headquarters until called into action, were placed in immediate reserve at intervals around the headquarters' building, and from there they were sent out.

Gale Brings New Havoc

The " raiders passed " came at 1-29 a.m. on Tuesday, December 24—Christmas Eve. By 3 a.m. every fire in the city had been completely surrounded with jets. Some of the fires were still burning fiercely, but the spread had been halted, and there was apparently no cause for undue concern. But at 3 o'clock fate took a hand. A strong north-easterly wind sprang up. It carried abroad sparks and burning embers, and swept them through the blast-shattered windows of warehouses and commercial buildings which had escaped destruction by the enemy. Within half an hour the battle was at its height again.

Danger threatened greatest in the Piccadilly area, where the insatiable flames already held giant warehouses in their grip. Pillars of fire reaching high into the sky turned night into day. From the outskirts of Manchester it looked as though half the city was ablaze. The sky glowed red.

As dawn broke the fiery furnace extended from Mosley Street across Piccadilly and beyond Portland Street. In depth, it threatened to penetrate almost as far as Princess Street. Many of the famed palaces of the merchant princes of past generations had already collapsed in blazing ruin. Many more were threatened with the same fate. Only drastic measures could save them.

An enemy's high explosives had touched them off; our own explosives would be their salvation. By blasting well-chosen buildings, a gap was cut in the path of the encroaching fire, and from pre-selected points powerful jets were brought to play, to beat the flames into subjection.

Men and women, boys and girls of the Manchester district were valiantly carrying on with their normal tasks—excited, maybe, from the effects of their experiences, but without grumble or complaint, when the rumble of blasting operations reverberated throughout the city.

Telephone Exchange Saved

In that vast blitz-cleared area which to-day extends behind the quiet gardens of Piccadilly a massive building—York House, hub of the Central telephone exchange—still stands erect. Popular conception is that it was saved by a providential twist of fate. In truth, it was saved by the herculean efforts of the fire services. So, too, were the electricity works in Dickinson Street which, though licked by flames, were saved from destruction.

Piccadilly was not the only awesome spectacle. Other grave fires were raging in Miller Street, in Victoria Street and St. Mary's Gate ; The Shambles, with all its colourful

THEATRES AND CINEMAS IN THE CITY ESCAPED SERIOUS DAMAGE, PERHAPS THE WORST-HIT BEING THE GAIETY, WITH THE ADJOINING CAFE ROYAL. BOTH WERE SOON OPEN AGAIN

and historic associations, was a mass of smoking ruins; 200 business houses, 165 warehouses, nearly 150 offices and five banks were destroyed or seriously damaged; more than 500 additional business houses, 20 banks, 300 warehouses and 220 offices suffered in lesser degree. Within a mile radius of Albert Square 31.3 acres had been laid in ruins.

Scores of famous and familiar buildings were no more than mere shells, or had disappeared entirely. Among them were the Free Trade Hall, Victoria Buildings, the Rates Offices, Cross Street Chapel, and the home of the Literary and Philosophical Society in George Street.

The Assize Courts escaped with only slight damage, to be destroyed in a later attack; the famous John Ryland's Library in Deansgate was slightly damaged; Chetham's Hospital and the Cathedral suffered grievously; the Masonic Temple, Corn Exchange Buildings, and St. Ann's Church had reeled under the blows of H.E.—but still stood, defiant. Hulme Town Hall and Library, Mayfield and Leaf Street Baths, the City Hall, Smithfield Market, all suffered serious injury.

Business houses whose names were of world-wide fame were reduced to ashes or scarred by flame and explosives. Among them were the Portland Street warehouses of A. & S. Henry, Ltd., Haslams, Ltd., Barlow & Jones, Ltd., S. & J. Watts & Co., J. F. & H. Roberts, Ltd., Armitage and Rigby, Ltd., S. Finburgh & Sons, Ltd.; of Sparrow Hardwick & Co., H. Bannerman & Sons, Ltd., Brookfield Aitchison & Co., Ltd., in York Street; Baxendale's extensive warehouses in Miller Street were reduced to desolation; the towering warehouses that flanked Parker Street—Peel, Watson & Co., J. Templeton & Co., and several others—were smouldering ruins.

School Hit Four Times

During the two nights of the blitz more than 100 school properties—municipal and non-provided—in Manchester alone suffered in more or less degree. Some were damaged so severely that repair was impossible. During the whole series of attacks the total number was 159.

It was a happier circumstance, however, that although so many school properties suffered damage or destruction, not a single pupil was in them at the time.

One school, in Southall Street, Cheetham, was damaged in four different raids; the new £90,000 Manchester High School for Girls was wrecked after the school had occupied the premises for only one term; incendiary bombs damaged the roof timbers of the Manchester School of Art; the Whalley Range High School for Girls suffered extensive damage, as also did the College of Domestic Economy and the hostel for its students.

In other raids the assembly hall and gymnasium of the Burnage High School for Boys were destroyed; Moseley Road School was damaged by a bomb which plunged through the roof; Chorlton Park School received extensive damage; one section of Old Moat School, Withington, was gutted; St. Joseph's Roman Catholic School in Plymouth Grove was wrecked; St. Oswald's Church of England School, Gorton Street, Collyhurst, was so severely damaged that it has not been possible to use it for school purposes since, and Atherton Street School, in the heart of the city, suffered grievous damage.

Two cinemas—the Futurist in Great Ducie Street, Strangeways, and the Victory Picture House in Charles Street, Blackley—were completely destroyed, four others were seriously damaged, and a dozen other places of entertainment suffered. No fewer than 23 public houses and breweries, including the Woolsack, the Falstaff, the famous Blue Boar Hotel and the Slip Inn in Blue Boar Court, the Old Millgate Hotel and the Coronation Hotel in Old Shambles, were destroyed; 22 others were seriously damaged, and 132 other well-known hostelries sustained lesser damage.

Within a few hours of the last serious fire being extinguished, leading officials were summing up the lessons of the blitz.

One thing they noted immediately was that a strengthening of the Fire Watchers' Order without delay was vital if the city were to be prepared adequately to face another such ordeal. It was a tragic truth that much of the devastation might have been prevented had sufficient fire watchers been on duty in many city warehouses and other premises, to douse the sparks and burning embers blown in through broken windows and damaged rooftops. No time was lost by the Manchester Emergency Committee in making suitable recommendations to the then Regional Commissioner.

30,000 Damaged Homes

The two-nights' blitz, however, had wrought havoc and destruction on a vast scale in Manchester and the surrounding localities. Scores of buildings had been blasted into ruins; others were reduced to shells, and many more were showing in lesser degree the scars of war. To that toll were added nearly 30,000 houses damaged in Manchester alone, and throughout the area several scores of thousands of people had been rendered homeless.

Military units were instantly called in to help cope with the situation and clear up the mess; members of the Home Guard mounted sentinel over many buildings, responding eagerly to the call of duty, even though in many cases they left their ruined homes behind them. Their presence was required not to restore, or even to maintain, order; their mission was one of succour. In that circumstance is found the most eloquent testimony to the courageous reactions of the " common people."

Manchester and its neighbours were not unprepared for the consequences of finding themselves in the front line. In Manchester, immediately the fires had subsided, 5,049 people who had been rendered homeless, or whose evacuation was deemed prudent because of the presence of unexploded bombs, had been found temporary communal shelter in 28 rest centres. There they were given blankets, food and replacements of lost and damaged clothing.

By January 2 the Manchester Corporation housing authorities had carried out first-aid repairs to approximately 13,000 houses within the city, and the work was still being pushed rapidly forward. Less than 1,600 people remained in the rest centres—and some of these had been found new homes but were waiting for transport to remove their salvaged furniture.

To feed the destitute multitude large catering concerns in Manchester were recruited. The authorities proved themselves quickly adaptable to the circumstances; after a few days hot meals were put on at night instead of at mid-day so that the worker could be sure of returning to his temporary " home " to a warm meal. In the first

20

BOMBED-OUT CHILDREN AT A CHRISTMA
PARTY IN A MISSION HALL, AND
HAPPY TRIO AT A NEW YEAR PARTY I
A STREET SHELTER. *Left:* ONE WHOS
HOME WAS DAMAGED BEING RECLOTHE
AT A VOLUNTARY WORKERS' CENTR

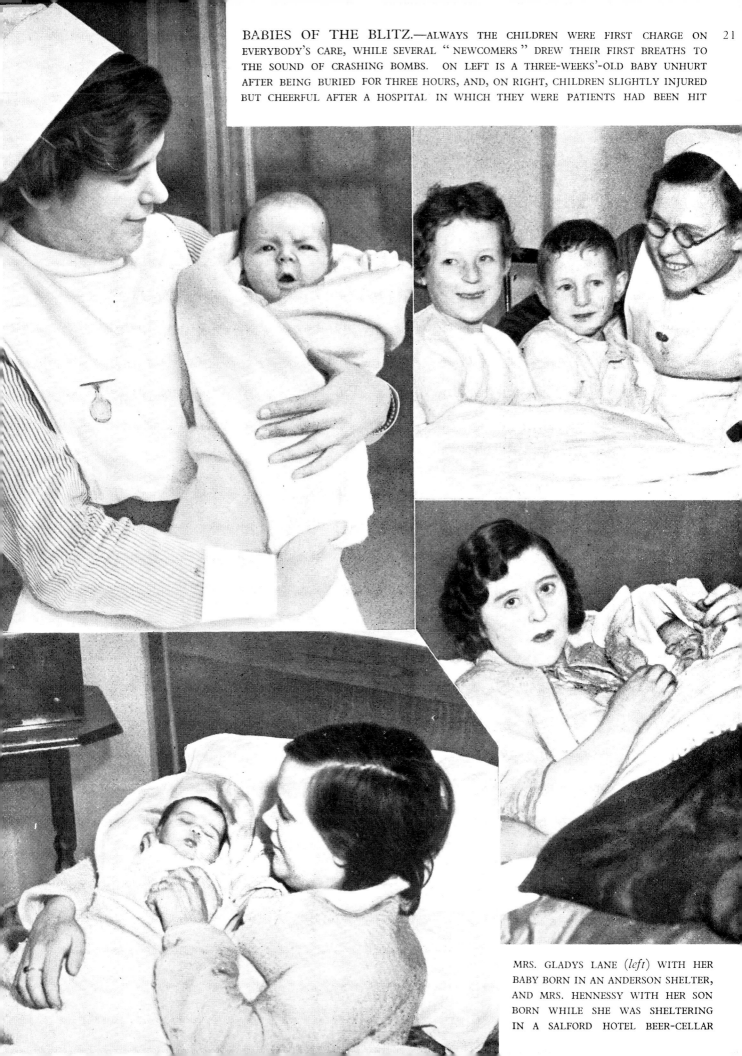

BABIES OF THE BLITZ.—ALWAYS THE CHILDREN WERE FIRST CHARGE ON EVERYBODY'S CARE, WHILE SEVERAL "NEWCOMERS" DREW THEIR FIRST BREATHS TO THE SOUND OF CRASHING BOMBS. ON LEFT IS A THREE-WEEKS'-OLD BABY UNHURT AFTER BEING BURIED FOR THREE HOURS, AND, ON RIGHT, CHILDREN SLIGHTLY INJURED BUT CHEERFUL AFTER A HOSPITAL IN WHICH THEY WERE PATIENTS HAD BEEN HIT

MRS. GLADYS LANE (*left*) WITH HER BABY BORN IN AN ANDERSON SHELTER, AND MRS. HENNESSY WITH HER SON BORN WHILE SHE WAS SHELTERING IN A SALFORD HOTEL BEER-CELLAR

eight days no fewer than 72,000 meals were served at the rest centres.

Simultaneously with these activities, the men and women still in the firing line—the firefighters, Civil Defence personnel and others—required to be fed. Along with many victims of the blitz, they were supplied with food from mobile canteens, many of them sent in by sympathetic neighbouring authorities; others had been provided by America, as a token of a then friendly neutral's admiration and affection. On one day alone the mobile canteens in Manchester fed 10,000 people.

The blitz had once and for all time dispelled the mild amusement with which some members of the populace were wont to regard some branches of the Civil Defence services—those men and women who, with no thought of self, but in a spirit of service, had assumed, in many cases, when the possibility of war seemed remote, the voluntary responsibility of attending to the needs and protection of their fellow men. They had won their laurels on the field of battle itself; some had won glory and honour in death; all had earned the gratitude and admiration of their fellow citizens.

In the city's dossier of secret reports on the blitz there is recorded a resolution of Manchester Emergency Committee which stands to their memory.

> *Your Committee considers*, it says, in cold, official and formal language, *that all services functioned magnificently, and is proud to be associated with an organisation, largely based on voluntary services, which signally distinguished itself when the time came.*
>
> *In the opinion of your Committee the citizens of Manchester suffered the effects of the raids with fortitude and determination of the highest character. At no stage was there any suggestion of panic, and the instructions of the police and Civil Defence services were carried out with courage and expedition.*
>
> *After the raid it was apparent that, in spite of the ordeal through which every one had passed, there was no feeling of helplessness, but a general desire to bring every effort to bear to restore normal conditions in the city so far as this was possible.*
>
> *The authorities have been greatly assisted by the manner in which individuals have busied themselves in first-aid repairs without waiting until official action was possible, and a general spirit of neighbourliness and mutual assistance has contributed largely to the speedy recovery from the effects of the raids.*
>
> *To all those organisations and individuals who have assisted in the maintenance of public morale in this way your Committee is deeply grateful.*

The report embodying that resolution was never made public. Security reasons required that the report should remain a secret document. We are pleased to record it, publicly, now.

SALFORD'S ORDEAL

FOR REASONS OF SECURITY it has not been possible until now to describe in detail the severity of the ordeal to which the people of Salford were subjected in the blitz. Not even the very human desire that their resistance to the enemy should be known and appreciated by their fellow countrymen was gratified, although the authorities made repeated efforts to have the story released.

For all the rest of the country knew, the city was never raided, never endured a blitz; yet few towns suffered such shattering damage, or fought the effects of high explosive and fire with such calm courage and high resolve. On the two nights of the blitz it is estimated that 276 high-explosive bombs and nearly 10,000 incendiaries fell within the boundaries of the city, causing one major conflagration, 31 major fires and 400 large, medium and minor fires, in addition to hundreds of house fires which were extinguished by police, wardens, and residents.

Altogether units and equipment of 59 outside fire services were rushed to the city, and by noon of December 24 the authorities were able to report that all fires were under control, and by dusk that the gigantic beacon the Nazi airmen had lighted was entirely subdued.

How much the gallantry and skill of Salford's defence services contributed to the relatively low total of casualties will never be known, but the toll, by any standard of reckoning, was not commensurate with the fury of the attack on a city whose crowded rows of very old property were fraught with the very highest degree of fire risk. The killed in the two nights numbered 197. One hundred and seventy-seven were seriously wounded, 648 slightly wounded, and in addition 18 members of police, fire and Civil Defence services lost their lives, and 85 were injured.

The measure of the devotion of the various services was finely expressed by the Inspector General of the Ministry of Home Security in a letter to the Mayor of Salford on January 10, 1941, in which he said : "We cannot know what the future may hold, but we have the utmost confidence that the Salford services will be ready for anything, and will maintain that high standard of efficiency they have set themselves." No praise was more worthily bestowed.

Indiscriminate Attack

The enemy's assault on the city followed no clear pattern. No particular industrial area was laid under bombardment more than another, and it may be said with authority that there was little pin-pointing of targets in the manner practised by the Allied bombers over Germany now. But this is certain, that the sombre length of the River Irwell was a welcome guide to the Nazi airmen.

The plight of citizens in the bombed area was pitiful in the extreme. More than 8,000 houses were destroyed or damaged in some way. The windows of 3,200 more were shattered by blast. Even in houses which escaped structural damage life was made hideous for weeks by a heavy grey film of dirt, smelling of death and destruction, which percolated through doors and crevices and taxed the patience of neat and tidy housewives as nothing had done in their lives before.

Though they had come unscathed through two nights of shattering noise, bursting bombs, and the lurid peril of engulfing fires, they forgot themselves and their sufferings in the misery of dirty homes. That was something for which they could never forgive Hitler—not if they lived to be a hundred years old.

In some areas life was complicated still further by temporary failure of the essential services. Gas holders, purifiers, retorts and distributing mains of the Corporation gas undertaking were so badly damaged by incendiary and high-explosive bombs that it became necessary, as a precaution against the suffocation of people trapped or working in debris, and against providing more guiding

COUNCIL CHAMBER WRECKED

WHEN A BOMB FELL BETWEEN THE SALFORD TOWN HALL AND A ROW OF HOUSES OPPOSITE THE COUNCIL CHAMBER WAS WRECKED, AND PEOPLE IN THE HOUSES HAD AMAZING ESCAPES. TWO OF THEM, IN BED AT THE TIME, SLITHERED DOWN THROUGH COLLAPSING BRICKS AND SLATES STILL ON THE MATTRESS, WHICH CAME TO REST IN THE CRATER WITH ITS ASTONISHED "PASSENGERS" PRACTICALLY UNHURT

CHRISTMAS BREAKFAST.—VANS
CONTAINING EMERGENCY FOOD SUPPLIES TOURED
THE WORST-HIT AREAS AFTER THE DECEMBER RAIDS.
BREAD BEING DELIVERED ON CHRISTMAS MORNING

beacons for the enemy, to cut off the supply to a number of districts. The network of electricity distributing mains was damaged, but not seriously, in twenty places, and 700 consumers were temporarily deprived of current. Happily, there was only the slightest interference with water supplies.

The " morning after " the raids, and, in some districts, for several mornings after, residents found themselves compelled to carry out an exercise never popular with city dwellers—walking to work. Throughout the city 139 roads were wholly or partially blocked by debris, but the delay in re-opening main roads to two-way traffic was negligible, and the clearing of less important roads and streets, though hampered by the presence of unexploded bombs, was carried through with unexampled speed and efficiency. One thousand five hundred soldiers were drafted into the city to help in this work, and they did yeoman service.

The Civil Defence workers of the city, like the personnel of all other bombed cities and towns, found that the terrors of the assault could best be sustained by hard and unremitting work. It was better to have a job to do than to wait, as many thousands were forced to do, for the bombs to fall. In swift and controlled execution of their tasks they found the perfect foil against nerve-strain and anxiety.

Heaven knows there was work enough for them to do. All the fixed First Aid Posts in the city were constantly in action. At Pendleton 101 casualties were treated ; at Blackfriars Road 88 ; at Regent Road 87 ; at Seedley 60—and this in spite of the fact that a number of the premises were damaged by bombs, and treatment of the injured had to be carried on by the feeble, uncertain light of candles and hurricane lamps. Not even the shattering explosion of bombs close by was allowed to interfere with the succouring of the victims.

First aid parties and ambulance teams carried on unflinchingly in the same conditions of horror, danger and difficulty.

Some of the Rescue Service squads had frightful experiences, but as fast as they were bombed from one depot they moved to another, so that the organisation, tested as it was almost to the limit of human endurance, continued to discharge its arduous and dangerous tasks. Quite early in the raid the central depot at Church Street, Pendleton, was damaged by a bomb, which destroyed and damaged a number of vehicles, threw the telephones out of action, and severely injured one of the super-intendents. Rescue squads at the Sewage Works and Wilburn Street were bombed out of their depots, but were promptly transferred to other stations. Their record is a shining page in the story of the selfless devotion of the Salford defence services. From the ruins of 86 buildings in the two nights they rescued alive 143 people who had been trapped by debris, and it was their melancholy duty to recover the bodies of 127 citizens who had been buried under the mountain of masonry which had once been their homes.

It is not surprising to read in the official report that, " having worked continuously day and night until late on December 24, some of the personnel gave way under the terrific strain." Time and again one reads that the work of the services was " magnificent." The list of awards for gallantry is testimony to the spirit which inspired them all—the police and special constabulary, the Warden's Corps, the Control Centre staffs, in addition to those whose work has already been mentioned.

The Report and Control Centre received and despatched during the attack no fewer than 3,300 messages, formal and dispassionate documents which no more than hinted at the anguish of a city. It was the swift appraisal of these messages, the perfect dovetailing of the services, and the prompt despatch of aid—all carried out in imminent danger and almost overwhelming discomfort — which saved the city from a disaster too terrifying, perhaps, to contemplate.

Police fought incendiaries in hundreds of streets, gave help to the injured, dug into craters and debris to rescue people who had been trapped, guided the homeless to the rest centres, marshalled the residents of many districts who had to leave their homes because of the danger of unexploded bombs, directed traffic—in short, behaved with the solid, heartening, irresistible efficiency which has made the British policeman the admiration of the world.

Calmness Never Failed

At no time during the attack was a single instance of panic, or even near-panic, reported. It was as if the people were clothed in a mantle of invulnerability, for their fortitude and calmness never failed. It is not detracting from their high courage to say that in some measure, at least, it was derived from the example set them by the police and the wardens with whom they shared a common peril.

Like the police, the wardens turned their hand to any task, however grim, which came their way. Voluntary service has found no higher expression that in the courage, zeal and all-round efficiency of the men and women who watched their own little communities with such untiring vigilance. After the raid 560 part-time wardens continued for some days to help in the work of succouring the people who had suffered in the attack.

The Corps of Messengers, a great majority of them young people, mustered more than 93 per cent of their available strength when the alert sounded on December 22.

They ran hundreds of urgent messages and extinguished scores of small fires without thinking they had performed any exceptional feat. This was the spirit which animated the city's services.

The vindictive hail of high-explosive and incendiary bombs inflicted grievous damage on the city's industrial premises, but the threat to its productive capacity was lessened by the extraordinary efforts of managements and workers. Within a few hours of the last bomb having fallen the restoration of damaged premises was put in hand. Repair gangs worked with prodigious speed to get machinery running again; office staffs and workpeople put up with the maximum of discomfort to maintain production at the highest possible level. Thousands went without sleep and food in sheer determination that Hitler should not be able to claim he had put them out of business.

The Nazis were never so wrong as when they imagined that a bomb on a building meant the end of production. In that premise they had not counted on the resource and foresight of executives, or the loyalty and fearlessness of workpeople. The later history of Salford industry proves how wrong the Germans were, and how meagre was the reward of their terrorism.

"Nerve Centre" Destroyed

Not all the bombs, of course, fell on buildings. Those which fell in the roads and streets disrupted tramway tracks and ripped overhead equipment from its supporting standards. This kind of damage, involving tedious and multitudinous repair jobs, was most serious in Oldfield Road, Trafford Road, Eccles New Road, Bolton Road, Regent Road and Lower Chapel Street, and one nerve centre of the transport service—the office at Pendleton—was completely demolished. Hundreds of public vehicles were damaged, and the cost of replacing shattered windows alone was prodigious. A bus standing under Greengate Arches was struck by falling debris, and a man and woman who had taken shelter in it were killed.

In an area so congested as Salford every bomb may be counted on to do damage. Perhaps it was this fact which dictated the bombing policy of the Nazi airmen. They hit or damaged every public bath in the city, though none was destroyed, and a stick of bombs which fell on Weaste Cemetery considerably damaged every chapel and wrought heartrending devastation among graves and memorials.

The Art Gallery at Peel Park lost scores of windows and roof lights, but its artistic treasures escaped injury. It was more fortunate than the Weaste branch library, where a near-by bomb-burst caused the collapse of a large part of the roof. Of the city's schools no fewer then 71 were damaged, nine of them very severely. Half of Pendleton (Charlestown) London Street School was demolished. There were direct hits on St. Joseph's R. C. boys', girls' and infants' schools. The girls' department of Stowell Memorial C. of E. School was demolished, and the boys' school heavily damaged.

A direct hit on Christ Church Upper C. of E. School partly demolished the building. One section of Weaste All Souls' R. C. School was destroyed by a bomb which fell in the school yard. The Junior Instruction Centre, Huddart Street, was a total loss. A large calibre bomb which fell near Weaste St. Luke's C. of E. School made the premises temporarily unsafe. The top floor of Tootal Road Council School was completely burned out.

Fifteen other schools were extensively damaged, and 47 suffered damage in less serious degree. In such manner was German *kultur* demonstrated to the boys and girls of Salford.

Looking at the blitz in retrospect it seems incontestable that no more poignant duty fell to the lot of any branch of the city's services than that which was carried out by the staffs of the rest centres. To these centres, in the space of a few days, came 12,000 people, most of them hollow-eyed from loss of sleep, pitifully silent from grief and anxiety about the fate of those near and dear to them, hungry, inadequately clothed, and, for the time being at least, homeless.

To these people kindness was as great a need as water to a dying man. It was given them in ungrudging measure. When three of the centres and two sub-centres were put out of action through bomb damage new ones were opened. When drivers of food lorries and vans found their way to the centres blocked by debris they explored other roads and made sweeping detours, but they never failed to fight their way through.

Four thousand people were cared for and fed on the first night of the blitz. Four thousand more came on the second night. After the attack there was another sad pilgrimage of people who had had to leave their homes through the discovery of unexploded bombs.

More than 80,000 meals which literally kept body and soul together in thousands of people were served in the rest centres of the city, a work of mercy and humanity for which no praise is too high. And side by side with

THE ODD CHANCE.—SHELTERING IN THIS BUS UNDER A RAILWAY ARCH, TWO PEOPLE WERE KILLED WHEN THE TRACK WAS PIERCED BY A BOMB

this duty ran the responsibility of finding homes for those who had lost everything. It was carried out with energy and compassion, and in an incredibly short time 18,000 people were billeted in the city or outside, in addition to 1,200 who found temporary homes with friends and relatives. New homes were found for 2,225 people.

This, then, is the story of Salford in the blitz. In it there must necessarily be many gaps, just as in battle the heroism of many soldiers must go unrecorded and unhonoured. The narrative may fitly be rounded off by quoting an extract from a letter to the Mayor of Salford by Wing-Commander G. S. Hodsoll, Inspector-General, Ministry of Home Security, who visited the city on January 10, 1941.

In his letter he said :

I was delighted to have a chance of visiting Salford again and meeting some of the Civil Defence workers. I should like to extend to them all my very warmest congratulations on the magnificent way in which they met their very severe tests.

I have watched the growth of the services in Salford from their beginning, and always had great confidence that they would be ready for anything that might come. The magnificent way in which they carried out their duties is a source of great pride, and has added to the prestige of the Civil Defence services, not only in Salford, but throughout the country.

STRETFORD

NOT MANY YARDS away from Stretford Town Hall, during the height of the blitz, a resident looked out from the porch of his house and saw a fantastic and horrific spectacle. He saw tall pillars of flame rearing up from incendiaries which had fallen in the fields near by. He saw the flames which licked hungrily at the pavilion and stands of the Lancashire County Cricket Ground. He saw the dull red glow which illuminated the clouds high over the heart of Manchester. He looked towards Chorlton, and saw more fires. Towards Salford, towards Stretford—everywhere fires.

THE COUNTY CRICKET GROUND HAS BEEN HIT BY BOTH HIGH-EXPLOSIVE AND INCENDIARY BOMBS. HERE IS A CRATER CLOSE TO THE TEST MATCH PITCH, WITH THE GROUNDSMAN LOOKING ON DISCONSOLATELY

He could hear the intermittent beat of the engines driving the Luftwaffe planes across the sky. From his vantage point he could hear the shattering salvos of the Ack-Ack guns, and he could follow the trail of sound as the deadly projectiles soared to the altitude set on their fuses.

Substantially the same spectacle might have been seen from a hundred different points, where open spaces permitted an all-embracing view. It was a sight to numb the senses and quench the spirit of resistance, if many months of training and an awareness of the peril which sooner or later had to be faced, had not brought out the finest qualities of the Civil Defence services and the residents.

Like Salford, Stretford has been denied until now the satisfaction of reading other than anonymously about its conduct in the attack. Like Salford, it faced peculiar dangers and overcame them with the same heroic spirit. The very heart of a great industrial zone, where vital war production is being carried on, is not the place in which many people would choose to live and face the fury of a remorseless enemy if they had been concerned only with their own safety.

Only by hard facts can the severity of the attack on Stretford be assessed. One hundred and forty-three high explosive bombs, many of the heaviest calibre, fell on the town in the two nights. Hundreds of incendiaries cascaded on the buildings, the homes of the inhabitants, and in the streets. Of the 106 people who lost their lives 10 were children. Eighty-seven people were seriously injured and detained in hospital, and 184 were slightly injured. The toll was mercifully light. Considering the widespread operations of the defence services, and the risks to which they were exposed, it was miraculously light.

During the first night two incidents occurred which added enormously to the difficulties of organisation. For two periods, amounting to more than four hours, the electricity supply to the Report Centre was interrupted, and the various officials and staffs which dealt with the flood of incoming reports had to carry on their work by the light of candles and hand-lamps.

The second incident was infinitely more serious. It might, indeed, have been disastrous if improvisation on a boldly imaginative scale had not been carried out. A bomb which destroyed the East Union Street police station, completely severed telephone communication with the Report Centre, and it was not possible to restore it during the attack. It also cut off the Report Centre from telephone communication with the Empress Street reserve ambulance depot, the Wright Street Rescue Party depot, and Manchester Town Hall, all of them of the greatest importance in the scheme of defence. The demands made upon the car and bicycle messenger services, and even foot messengers, were, in consequence, stepped up out of all proportion to what had been expected of them ; nevertheless, the telephone isolation was countered, and the " front line " organisation continued to function with the highest efficiency.

Five police officers were killed in the East Union Street Station, which was the headquarters of an extensive Lancashire County police division, and three others were injured. It is worth emphasizing that in a very short time the police organisation was fully restored in alternative headquarters previously prepared near by. A potential breach in the defences had been averted by foresight and preparedness.

On both nights of the raid the police and wardens were greatly helped by the zeal with which residents tackled incendiaries which fell on, or near, their homes. The " scratch " stirrup-pump teams, uncertain, perhaps, in their first approach to the task, were veteran firefighters before the raid was over.

But the main burden was borne by the defence workers, and the distinction with which they performed their tasks and their devotion to duty—giving " duty " the widest possible interpretation—is shown by the award of two George Medals, ten British Empire Medals, three M.B.E.'s and five Commendations to members of the various branches of the services.

The record of damage was not so formidable as at Salford, but many public buildings were destroyed or damaged. Among them were :

The Town Hall (slightly)
Lancashire County Cricket Ground
Stretford High School for Girls
Henshaw's Institution for the Blind
Globe Cinema, Old Trafford
Welsh Church, Old Trafford
Old Trafford Baths, Northumberland Road
Unitarian Church, Old Trafford
St. Peter's Church, Gorse Hill
St. Joseph's R. C. School
County Police Headquarters, Old Trafford
Ministry of Labour Employment Exchange, Brunswick Street
Victoria Park Council School Shelters
All Saints' Church
Lostock School
Park Road Post Office
Metropolitan-Vickers Club, Moss Road
Corona Cinema
White City Greyhound Track

As in all other bombed towns, it was the homes of the people which took the greater weight of the bombs showered down by the warplanes of the enemy. The toll was particularly heavy. More than 12,000 houses were either destroyed or damaged. The occupiers of hundreds more houses continued to live for some time

NOT SO GRAND.—ONE OF THE STANDS AT THE MANCHESTER UNITED FOOTBALL GROUND. THE RIVAL " CITY " PROMPTLY CAME TO THE RESCUE, HELPING THE CLUB OVER ITS DIFFICULTIES BY SHARING ITS GROUND

afterwards in conditions of the greatest discomfort because of broken windows.

Even this does not complete the record of hardship borne with exemplary fortitude by the people of Stretford. During the attack all the utility services—gas, water and electricity—received severe damage, and fourteen days elapsed before the blessing of warmth, light and water from the kitchen tap was wholly restored to the inhabitants.

Although more than 2,000 people who had lost their homes, or had been evacuated because of the menace of unexploded bombs, were able to find shelter with relatives or friends, as many again were cared for at the rest centres, conducted by personnel of the Women's Voluntary Services. Much of the sorrow of these unfortunate people was assuaged by the kindliness with which they were treated.

THE OUTER AREAS

MORE THAN THREE YEARS after the great attack on the Manchester area officials charged with the defence of STOCKPORT still ask themselves : " How did we escape so lightly ? " It is a sombre question ; and he who seeks the answer may find it in the courage and readiness of its citizens.

It is not to be denied that of all the towns in greater Manchester, Stockport was, perhaps, the most fortunate. Lying on one of the two main assault routes of the Luftwaffe into Manchester, at a point where enemy raiders felt the first fierce impact of the anti-aircraft defences, the borough might conceivably have paid heavily for its geographical situation. The defence organisations and the public had indeed braced themselves for an assault no less violent than that which fell on Manchester, Salford and Stretford.

For one brief period early in the second night of the blitz there was a possibility that these forebodings might be realised. From enemy planes flying many thousands of feet above the town thousands of incendiaries were

THE KING AND QUEEN PAID TRIBUTE TO THE ENDURANCE OF THE CITIZENS WHEN THEY PAID A VISIT IN FEBRUARY, 1941. HERE THEY ARE INSPECTING MANCHESTER NURSES

Stockport were made. Although H.E. bombs and several thousand incendiaries were dropped, only four people were killed, two seriously injured, and eighteen slightly injured. Material damage was on a equally low scale, some hundreds of houses being damaged, of which only twenty-three were totally destroyed.

Not one major "incident" was reported, and the luckiest escape was at the Alice Briggs Remand Home, Didsbury Road, where some time previously a heavy bomb had caused a deep crater near the shelters in the grounds. On the first night of the "blitz" another bomb, also of heavy calibre, demolished the buildings, but did not harm the boys in the shelters.

An H.E. fell in the playground of St. George's School, Buxton Road, causing some damage to the school and seriously impeding the work of a first aid centre in the adjoining St. George's Church. The personnel carried on in spite of the difficulties. At Heaton Norris goods station a heavy bomb damaged property, but not a single person was hurt, and even a number of horses in the stables survived without injury.

THE KING PAYS TRIBUTE

suddenly released. They fell in Davenport, Heaton Mersey, in the Town Centre, Heaton Moor, Offerton and Reddish, and observers on high ground saw hundreds of fires flickering in the darkness—some in the homes of the people, some in gardens, but the great majority on open ground.

Half an hour later, when bombers carrying high explosives passed over the town, questing, presumably, for tell-tale fires, Stockport lay darkly quiet beneath the winter sky, its fires extinguished, its personnel standing by for any new "incidents" which might be reported.

There can be no doubt that the town was saved from an attack of much greater violence and severity by the skill, energy and promptness with which the A.F.S., police, wardens, Home Guards and civilians tackled the scattered fires. An official of the Corporation has placed on record his experiences of a journey into town during that vital half-hour. "Every few yards there was an incendiary burning," he said. "I saw figures silhouetted against the flames, eagerly pumping water or throwing earth on them. I did not see a solitary blaze which was not being fought."

There was an elderly woman, living in a remote part of the town, who was seen to crawl many yards on muddy ground to beat down the flames which threatened her own little home.

This was the stuff of which the men and women of

When the count of damage became known next day, not the least angry residents were members of Heaton Moor Golf Club, who found the fairways and almost every green scarred by the burning of hundreds of incendiaries.

HIS MAJESTY HALTS DURING HIS TOUR OF SALFORD'S DAMAGED AREAS TO TALK TO A CIVIL DEFENCE NURSE

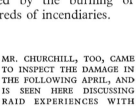

MR. CHURCHILL, TOO, CAME TO INSPECT THE DAMAGE IN THE FOLLOWING APRIL, AND IS SEEN HERE DISCUSSING RAID EXPERIENCES WITH MANCHESTER WARDENS

ON the night of December 22, 1940, a happy Christmas party was in full swing at a house in Gilda Brook Road, ECCLES, used as a First Aid Depot. First-aid personnel were the hosts, and friends and relatives, with some children, were guests.

The party had begun early, and, because of the danger of raids, it had been planned to break up early. The partings were not early enough, for at quarter-past seven a heavy bomb exploded in the roadway, very close to the building, and twelve people were killed or died of their injuries. Nine of them were members of the First Aid Party. Every one of the remaining thirty-one people was either injured or suffered shock.

In the house next door a husband and wife and their three children were killed by the same bomb. It may be that heavier bombs fell in the Manchester area during the blitz, but there were few which took such heavy toll, or whose tally of destruction was attended by such harrowing circumstances.

HOMES ARE TARGETS

WHEN THESE TWO HOUSES IN MANCHESTER WERE DEMOLISHED BY BLAST FROM A NEAR-BY BOMB, THEIR ROOFS, UNSUPPORTED, STILL HELD TOGETHER

Almost every person at the party was known to the Rescue Squads, who for five days fought their way through great piles of debris to bring succour to the injured and to recover the bodies of the dead. This was the most terrible experience the Civil Defence services were called upon to face in the attack. There were other bombs and other incidents, but none so tragic as this. Nor were there any which caused greater incon-

THE OCCUPANTS OF THIS PRESTWICH HOME HAD REMARKABLE ESCAPES. THEY WERE SHELTERING UNDER THE STAIRCASE, AND WERE RESCUED BADLY SHAKEN BUT UNHURT

AN ANDERSON SHELTER ONLY A FEW YARDS AWAY SAVED A FAMILY WHEN THIS SALE HOUSE WAS HIT

venience to the residents of the district. The road remained closed many weeks, blocked by the crater and unusable through difficult and tedious repairs to sewers, and water, gas and electricity mains.

In Monton Road another heavy bomb, by evil chance, fell on a house to which had come as visitor a sailor home on leave from the battleship *Queen Elizabeth*. He and three children of the house, aged sixteen, twelve and six were killed. Thus, two incidents alone accounted for the majority of the victims of the attack on Eccles, and of the eighteen seriously and twenty-four slightly injured nearly half were at the ill-fated Gilda Brook Road party. Many more H.E. bombs and showers of incendiaries fell in the town—Wellington Road, Regent Street, Monton Road and Ellesmere Avenue were, perhaps, the hardest hit—but the loss of life was in no way commensurate with the damage to property. More than 1,400 houses were damaged to some extent in the blitz, including a small number demolished, and the occupiers of many hundreds more houses were called upon to endure as stoically as they might the discomforts of living in homes without windows.

Nothing shows up more clearly the utter abandon with which the Nazi raiders unloaded their bombs than the fact that not a single important building or business concern was put out of action, and, indeed, very few were hit at all. In parts of the town gas supplies were interrupted

THE HOUSEWIFE EXAMINES THE CRATER MADE BY A BOMB THAT DEMOLISHED HER HOME AT STOCKPORT. THE FAMILY ESCAPED

for a few hours, and there was some damage to water mains, and electricity and telephone services, but the Civil Defence services, extended as they were, were able by their own courageous and skilful efforts to restrict the damage.

The warm humanity displayed by the authorities in dealing with the homeless and with temporarily-evacuated families gained its own reward in gratitude and goodwill, and in the maintenance of high public morale. There are in the files at the Town Hall to-day many letters, written in the throes of great emotion. But the sentiments they expressed more than three years ago are still held by those who wrote them.

To find virtually under one roof all the help and advice and material aid they needed, as they did because the authorities had arranged it so, was a godsend to all of them. Thanks to the enlightened control of the administrative departments of the Corporation the people of Eccles returned to new homes and to their jobs sooner then they had ever dared to hope.

A FEW weeks after the attack on SWINTON and PENDLEBURY, the Town Clerk, writing with full and intimate knowledge of the events and incidents of those dark hours, made these comments in a report to the Air Raid Precautions Committee :

The inhabitants of Swinton and Pendlebury took the attack in the same spirit as the unfortunate people in other parts of the country, and I am satisfied that these attacks of the enemy have only stiffened the determination of the townspeople to see this dreadful war brought to a successful conclusion, and thus put an end to the dictatorships which have arisen in Europe in recent years.

The Town Clerk expressed his admiration for the manner in which the homeless had taken the attack made upon them. " Although we had more than 1,000 people homeless and hundreds of houses damaged," he wrote, " I did not receive one complaint from the people who suffered."

The people to whom this glowing tribute was paid were under fire within a few minutes of the alert on December 22nd. They had barely time to reach the shelters, or to report to their posts of duty, before the intense white radiance of Nazi flares lay over the town. The assault heralded developed quickly. High explosives followed showers of incendiaries in the approved Nazi technique.

Trapped in Surface Shelter

A heavy bomb wrecked property in Hopwood Street and Bridge Street and demolished two surface shelters. From the debris the Rescue Party, by herculean efforts, rescued all but two of the people trapped, and they recovered the bodies of the victims the next day. More houses were shattered by bomb bursts in Gladstone Street and Lottie Street. In Agecroft Road a bomb fractured two water mains and spread flood water deeply over the road.

Public shelters off Agecroft Road, happily unoccupied, were damaged. Two houses in Park Lane West were hit, and blast damaged many more.

Several people were killed by a heavy bomb in St. Mary's Terrace, Dawson Street, but the toll of life was otherwise astonishingly light, not a single person being injured in a series of incidents in May Road, Blantyre Road, East Drive and Temple Lodge Estate.

Of the scores of incidents on the first night of the attack only a small proportion involved loss of life or even injury, and interference with the town's part in the war effort was negligible. Rarely, indeed, have Nazi raiders squandered their bombs to such little effect. The brunt of the assault, as in all other bombed cities and towns, was borne by the homes of the people. If it had been borne with less fortitude and less courage the Nazis might truly have struck a more flattering balance sheet. Even after a lapse of more than three years there is a grim satisfaction to be found in saying that, apart from some pitiful and futile destruction, the reward of the attack was nil.

Saved By Table

The ordeal of the night of December 23—24 was much less severe, although a number of serious incidents called for the highest degree of co-operation and skill by the various defence services. At the corner of Ashdown Avenue and Barton Road four people were trapped in a shop. When the rescue workers reached them they found the husband dead, and his wife and two children unhurt beneath the kitchen table.

A bomb of the heaviest calibre demolished three houses and wrecked many others in Kingsway, but three people who were trapped in a house were rescued uninjured. A private shelter close by was damaged by blast. The only victim was a woman, who was found dead in the entrance. Three people inside the shelter were safe.

All the defence services came through the ordeal with the consciousness of a duty well done. They had dealt with scores of incidents in an attack which had cost more than twenty lives and injury to a number of other people, and neither in organisation nor in personal skill and courage when at grips with the enemy's fell work had they fallen below the standard expected of them.

The after-the-blitz operations were carried out with equal efficiency. Blocked roads were cleared; public services were restored in most affected areas in a very short time; rest centres were opened; repairs to damaged houses were put in hand. Meals were provided, and on Christmas Day, when it was found that the supply of gas to the more important bakeries could not be re-established in time, a disquieting shortage of bread was made good by the wholehearted co-operation of bakers outside the town's boundary, rallied to their aid by Swinton officials.

With the same promptness, and in every aspect of humanity and kindness, the homeless were found accommodation which would serve till they could return to their own or new homes.

Reception Area Hit

IT was, perhaps, ironical that the ALTRINCHAM district, which had given refuge to some hundreds of evacuees from the more congested industrial neighbourhoods in the early days of the war, should find itself in the battle line during the great December blitz on the Manchester area.

Altrincham had welcomed the children—and many of their parents, too—from the danger areas. Yet the bombs and incendiaries which fell upon the ancient market town during those December nights destroyed completely sixteen houses and damaged in varying degrees many other dwellings. The blitz cost the lives of twelve local inhabitants and injuries to a number of others.

MANY of the recognised appliances now used for dealing most effectively with the incendiary bomb were the inevitable outcome of the fire raids with which the enemy attacked us. But before they were invented northerners were not slow to improvise the quickest method of handling the fire bombs.

After the December blitz many were the local police and special police in SALE who reported back to their stations with their capes badly burnt or scorched. The explanation was simple. Policemen found they had no other weapons with which to tackle the incendiary bombs which were showered over several parts of the district, so they whipped off their cloaks and smothered the bombs with them.

Town Hall Ablaze

Many fires were reported in the Sale district during the night of December 23-24, but the local services prevented them causing any serious damage. There was one exception. Incendiaries struck the Town Hall. The fires got a grip on the building, and ultimately the council chamber and the clock tower were destroyed. But long before dawn had broken every fire was either extinguished or well under control.

About a dozen people were injured by a stick of H.E. which straddled the district on the first night of the blitz. Three of them demolished houses and another dropped in the centre of the Sale Rugby Football ground. On the second night, when ten more people suffered injury, H.E. bombs fell harmlessly on a corporation tip, though one bomb caused some damage to the Bridgewater Canal embankment.

Sale suffered casualties in other raids, but in not a single instance did they prove fatal. In that respect Sale's record was unique.

END HOUSES OF SEVERAL STREETS JOINED TOGETHER IN ONE CONTINUOUS MOUND OF RUBBLE WHERE A BOMB FELL. THE GLASS IN THE STREET LAMP WAS UNBROKEN

WHEN
THE
CITY
BURNED

ROADWAYS DRENCHED FROM THE FIREMEN'S HOSES AND LITTERED WITH BROKEN GLASS CAST MYRIAD REFLECTIONS FROM BLAZING BUILDINGS. LOOKING ALONG HANGING DITCH IN THE EARLY HOURS OF DECEMBER 23, 1940

SMOKE BILLOWING FROM THE TOP OF THE ROYAL EXCHANGE TOWER. BELOW IT A LARGE AREA OF THE WORLD-FAMOUS "FLOOR" HAD COLLAPSED, BUT TEMPORARY REPAIRS SOON MADE IT POSSIBLE FOR MEMBERS TO CONDUCT "BUSINESS AS USUAL"

"WINGED WITH RED LIGHTNING AND IMPETUOUS RAGE"

ON THE MORNING of December 23, 1940, the tide of
workers which flows into Manchester through
Piccadilly saw what was probably the biggest
blaze ever witnessed in England since the Great Fire of
London in 1666.

Within a week London burned again, and the great
fire of Manchester was eclipsed, but while it raged it
covered nine and a quarter acres of offices, business
premises and warehouses, destroying thousands of miles
of cloth and causing damage which can almost certainly
be reckoned in millions.

Piccadilly and its twin channels, Portland Street and
Mosley Street, are the mercantile heart of the cotton
trade of Manchester. Acre after acre is covered with
warehouses, a name which here implies something more
than the storehouses which are called warehouses else-

where. They are really vast wholesale shops, with
customers in all corners of the globe. As such, Portland
Street, in particular, was, on December 22, 1940, the
most dignified street in the city.

It remained so until the early hours of that dark
Tuesday when, towards the end of their second blitz on
Manchester, the enemy dropped both high explosives and
incendiaries near Piccadilly. When the earliest workers
came to town it did not seem particularly serious, but
when the 8-30 a.m. crowds arrived in the " fag-end " of
the black-out they saw a vast sheet of flame stretching
across the southern side of Manchester's great square.

The sombre and the lurid were equal partners in this
scene. The significance of it all was not lost on the
crowds. They did not say much ; after a wondering
pause most of them passed on to their jobs haunted by

BACK PICCADILLY, ABLAZE FROM END TO END;
MOST SPECTACULAR FIRE IN| MANCHESTER'S HISTORY

the question : Would it be possible to repel that mighty blaze before it reached the natural fire-breaks of Princess Street and even Oxford Street ? If it ever got so far the mercantile greatness of Manchester would be shattered for a term.

For the gallant firefighters of Manchester, Salford and the towns that had come to their assistance this blaze was the crowning ordeal. It came at the end of a two days' visitation when they were tired in body—though not in courage—from many hours of effort all round the twin cities, when water-pressure was reduced, and before auxiliary supplies could be relayed from neighbouring canals. But they tackled this rapidly-spreading inferno courageously, police, firemen and civilians risking, and sometimes losing, their lives from high explosives.

The fire was fiercest in the Parker Street area, but as the morning wore on warehouse after warehouse was engulfed, damaged or threatened. Among them were many whose names are known throughout the world—firms which to successive generations had seemed as immovably safe as the Bank of England. Indeed, there are in the streets which radiate from Piccadilly firms which are even older than that symbol of English stability.

Among those whose premises were destroyed or damaged in varying degrees were Barlow & Jones's, Peel Watson's, Sparrow Hardwick's, A. & S. Henry's, Haslams, J. F. & H. Roberts's, J. Templeton's, Brookfield Aitchison's, S. & J. Watts's, and S. Finburgh's.

The murderous blaze, which swept right along the square and began to eat deeply into the hinterland, was helped on its career by wind and by bomb-blast which had broken windows through which sparks gained a ready

35

AS THE FLAMES DIED DOWN
IN PICCADILLY, AND THE
INTERIORS OF BUILDINGS
COLLAPSED ONE AFTER
ANOTHER, THE FLAMES FOUND
FRESH FUEL AS THEY SPREAD
ALONG PORTLAND STREET
(*above*) AND MOSLEY STREET

THE BURNING ENTRANCE
HALL AND OFFICES AT
EXCHANGE STATION

entry. The antiquity of many of the buildings helped the fire no less than the immense stores of cloth. It was a bad look-out for any building into which flame penetrated.

Quickly it was realised that if the heart of Manchester were to be saved drastic measures would have to be taken. The Royal Engineers arrived and could be seen making their way down the streets filled with smoke, murk, steam, fallen and falling masonry. There was nothing for it but to dynamite a break. That is always a difficult decision, for it entails destroying buildings as yet untouched.

At last the charges were laid and the dull boom of explosives began. The fire had now to jump a man-made chasm to continue its destruction. It paused, and gradually fell back. The great fire of Manchester was checked. It flared fitfully behind its screen of empty window-frames and fantastically fallen buildings, guttering and smouldering as Christmas came.

The menace to the mercantile core of Manchester had been stopped in mid-course, and spectators saw that the vast, fortress-like warehouse of S. & J. Watts, most remarkable of its kind in England, still stood. It was not fanciful to see in it a symbol of the staunchness of Manchester in its most threatened hour.

While the damage was overwhelmingly to warehouses, there was one notable exception among the victims. Hidden in George Street, in a fine old eighteenth-century house, a relic of the days when the neighbourhood was the residential hub of Manchester, was the headquarters of Manchester's Literary and Philosophical Society, second in age only to the Royal Society. In it were preserved, until fire destroyed them, the apparatus used by the great Dalton in formulating the Atomic Theory and the *secretaire* used by the even greater Newton, together with relics or mementoes of scientists like Joule, who revolutionised nineteenth-century physics. These men enlarged the human mind, which Germany sought, but failed, to cow with fire and steel.

TRAGIC REMINDER OF SOMEBODY'S HOME—A BATTERED THREE-PIECE SUITE AND A PIANO KEYBOARD—AMONG THE COLLECTION AT A MANCHESTER SALVAGE DUMP

HEROISM OF THE HOSPITALS

By H. J. BRADLEY

TWISTED BUT STILL RECOGNISABLE, A ROOF, COMPLETE WITH ITS DORMER WINDOWS, SETTLES DOWN TO
COVER THE WRECKAGE OF FOUR STOREYS OF MASONRY, EQUIPMENT, AND FURNITURE NOW COLLAPSED
INTO ONE COMPACT HEAP OF RUBBLE AT THE VICTORIA MEMORIAL JEWISH HOSPITAL, MANCHESTER

WHETHER BY ACCIDENT OR DESIGN the waves of enemy bombers which swept over Manchester and Salford in Christmas week, 1940, left few of the famous hospitals in the twin cities undamaged. It is, indeed, difficult to believe that the attacks upon them were not systematic, a conviction strengthened by the fact that in other raids on the district hospitals were singled out, notably Salford Royal, where a direct hit killed fourteen nurses.

On the nights of December 22 and 23, however, the principal victims were Manchester Royal Infirmary and Nurses' Home, the Manchester Victoria Memorial Jewish Hospital, the Royal Eye Hospital, Hope Hospital, and Hacking's Nursing Home (the oldest in Manchester).

Others damaged included Salford Royal Hospital; the Manchester Children's Hospital, Gartside Street; the Dental School and Hospital, Cambridge Street; the Manchester Ear Hospital, Lower Ormond Street; the Central Branch of the Royal Infirmary, commonly known to Mancunians simply as Roby Street; and both blocks of St. Mary's Hospital for Women and Children at Whitworth Park and Whitworth Street West in the city area.

In these widespread attacks members of the medical, nursing and administrative staffs paid with their lives for their devotion to duty. Without exception they and their colleagues had done their best for their patients who, having been moved to shelters or emergency quarters, were found to be uninjured when the tally was taken.

A very notable example of this is afforded by the story of Hope Hospital, Salford, where as the result of a direct hit the hospital lost at once almost the flower of its staff. Six of them, including the medical superintendent and the matron, were killed, together with the medical superintendent's wife, the head porter, the head plumber, and the steward's wife.

All services—heat, light, water and telephone—were destroyed, together with the offices, books and records. Yet not one patient suffered more than minor abrasions and shock. Moreover, the work of the hospital went bravely on. In the operating theatre emergency operations continued; grammar school boys working in

AND 14 NURSES DIED

SCENES AT SALFORD ROYAL HOSPITAL AFTER THE RAID IN WHIT-WEEK, 1941, WHEN 14 NURSES WERE KILLED

CIVIL DEFENCE WORKERS REMOVING DEBRIS AND (*left*) RESCUING, AFTER ELEVEN HOURS' WORK, A TRAPPED NURSE

VIEWING THEIR WRECKED RECREA-
TION ROOM AT THE MANCHESTER
INFIRMARY NURSES' HOME AFTER
A RAID DURING OCTOBER, 1940

MANCHESTER

ROYAL

INFIRMARY

THE INFIRMARY SUFFERED AGAIN
A FEW MONTHS LATER, WHEN
ONE OF THE TWO 100 - FOOT
TOWERS WAS PARTLY DEMOLISHED

stretcher parties stuck to their posts, and nurses and staff evacuated patients—a task which went on until some eight hundred were sent home or to other institutions.

With the control staff killed, the steward, knowing that his wife lay dead beneath the debris, carried on until morning manning an emergency control and supervising the breakfasts of the staff and nurses. It is such devotion which explains why, within two days, Hope was standing by with beds ready for further casualties. By the end of the month it was already admitting and treating urgent cases again.

Very similar in spirit are the combined narratives of what happened when the Manchester Victoria Memorial Jewish Hospital was hit on the night of December 22, leaving the nurses' home near the hospital badly damaged. Again the patients were in the shelters and escaped. Not so the staff. Five of them were killed and three injured. But doctors, staff and rescuers worked on, performing urgent operations and struggling to release people trapped in the nurses' home,

When daylight came the Hospital had to be evacuated to Crumpsall, and was out of commission until workmen strutted bulging walls and repaired damaged ceilings and so forth.

Manchester Royal Infirmary had to endure a number of visitations from Nazi bombs, one of which destroyed the new Nurses' Home and its contents. During the big blitz the Infirmary lost many of its windows from blast, while a delayed-action bomb fell outside and, exploding later, caused considerable damage.

But here again, during Goering's biggest attempt to cripple Manchester, there was not a single casualty among the patients, some of whom wrote to the Lord Mayor of Manchester praising the conduct of the nurses who, though flung about by high explosive falling outside, pressed on with their duties. Two of them, undeterred by smoke and heat, smothered an incendiary bomb which fell down a chimney and burnt fiercely on the hearth of one of the men's wards.

The bombing of Manchester's Royal Eye Hospital was heavy, dramatic, and the cause of much material havoc. Four wards were hit, including a new £10,000 private patients' ward. Completed only a few days before the attack, it was left a total wreck.

Here, the force of the explosion extended even to a shelter, where a doctor was killed. A collapsing floor caused fatal injuries to a nurse; two patients were blown

ROOFLESS REFUGE.—THIS BUILDING, ONE OF THE GROUP COMPRISING HOPE HOSPITAL, PENDLETON, WAS THAT SET ASIDE AS AGED PEOPLE'S HOMES

into the road outside and another doctor was pinned underground by a mass of debris.

Two patients, a policeman and an aircraftman, were admitted to the hospital during the early part of the blitz suffering from eye injuries. But on hearing that the doctor was trapped they formed a rescue squad of their own, tunnelled through a two-foot wall, cleared a passage, and gradually levered the doctor to safety.

This hospital had to be evacuated for three months to Nell Lane Hospital, Withington, which had its own, if smaller, share of attention from the Luftwaffe. A single high-explosive bomb did considerable damage, a ward sister and a staff nurse suffering injuries.

On the night of the 23—24 December the only remaining casualty receiving hospital in Salford—Salford Royal—was put out of action by blast from a heavy bomb. Steps were at once taken to divert casualties to Crumpsall— and it is worthy of record that every call received at a First Aid Party and Ambulance Depot was answered, and in no case were personnel or vehicles found wanting.

Inside the hospital the few patients who were too ill to be moved were saved by the wire-glass protection on the windows, and two urgent operations were actually performed by the light of emergency lamps while the raid was in progress.

But Salford Royal's sternest ordeal came six months later, in June, 1941, when, as already mentioned, fourteen nurses were killed—the biggest single loss in all the enemy's attacks on our centres of healing. To-day the heroic nurses are commemorated by tablets, unveiled in February, 1944, by the Duchess of Kent, and by beds endowed from a £14,500 memorial fund raised by public subscription.

One well-known medical landmark whose long record of work in Manchester was ended by the blitz was Hacking's Nursing Home, close to the Royal Infirmary. In the very heavy bombing the matron was killed, together with a nurse and one patient. Most of the patients had to be freed from cellars buried beneath piles of bricks and beams.

One thing that should never be forgotten in the story of our hospitals in the blitz is the aid given by the assembly of large numbers of part-time volunteers. Many of them brought their own cars, and all worked hard and bravely during these nights of danger.

THE "FLOOR."—DEMOLITION WORKERS CLEARING UP THE DEBRIS AFTER THE FIRE AT THE ROYAL EXCHANGE, HEART OF LANCASHIRE'S COTTON INDUSTRY

"GINGER" STAYS PUT!

DEAF TO THE KINDLY COAXING OF WARDENS, "GINGER" A CAT BELONGING TO MRS SOPHIA WINTERS, REFUSED TO LEAVE ITS BOMBED HOME. MRS. WINTERS WAS KILLED, AND HER FOUR CHILDREN WERE INJURED. "GINGER" HAD ALREADY BEEN BOMBED OUT OF A PREVIOUS HOME.

ELAINE AND ANN SHAWCROSS, RETURNING FROM THEIR SHELTER TO THE PARTLY-DEMOLISHED DINING-ROOM OF THEIR HOME IN SALE, FOUND THEIR PET "BUDGIE" CHATTERING AWAY AS THOUGH NOTHING HAD HAPPENED.

A FIREFIGHTER EFFECTS A RESCUE—ANOTHER BUDGERIGAR—FROM A WRECKED HOUSE AT STOCKPORT.

THE CATHEDRAL—AND ITS FUTURE

By Dr. GARFIELD WILLIAMS
(Dean of Manchester)

I HAVE been asked to write something about the night of Sunday, the 22nd of December, 1940. Perhaps I should not have complied with this request had it not been that I feel I have a debt of honour to repay to Mr. Mulligan, the journalist who makes it.

Early on the morning of Monday, December 23, 1940, he found me among the ruins of my Cathedral. He did not pester me with questions. He just stood there with me. As he left me he said : " Is there anything I can do to help ? "

At first I think I said : " No." Then I said : " On second thoughts I think, perhaps, there is. I don't expect we shall be able to send any telegrams from Manchester to-day. My wife is down in Devonshire. She may hear of the destruction that has befallen the Cathedral and she will know that I was near at hand when it happened. Can you get some message to her that I am safe and well ? " He said he would do his best. As a matter of fact, he got a telegram through to her from Blackpool that day which set her mind at rest.

I had that Christmas week taken up my abode in the Victoria Hotel. My bedroom there was one of those in the curved portion of that building which at that time overlooked the Cathedral. Where it was then situated is now an empty space.

Somewhere about 6-30 on the night of December 22, my attention was distracted by a most curious noise—like fireworks exploding—and apparently it came from immediately outside my bedroom window. There had been no siren (or, at any rate, I had not heard one), but something told me at once what it was. It was the noise of incendiaries, and this was an air raid. Then I heard the 'planes.

Premature Optimism

In a few minutes I had all my things thrown into my two bags and was taking them to the office on the ground floor. As I went down the stairs somebody passed me the word that incendiaries had dropped on our roof. I followed my informant up aloft. It was curiously silent there.

Then I discovered that the trouble was in fact located in another, and distant, part of that amazing building. The information was that two incendiaries had been put out, but that a third had got into an angle of the roof where it could not be got at, and in that place fire was getting a hold on the roof. Just then a hose and auxiliary firemen appeared at the top of the stairs. It seemed to me that that was quick work, and I felt optimistic.

That emotion, however, was very premature, for it soon appeared that there was no water for the hose, nor, so far as I can remember, did any come through until it was too late for it to do any good. Certainly we got some water eventually, for by midnight we were driven out of the place far more by water than by fire, for the fire, burning from above downwards, made comparatively slow progress. The water came down those stairs like a Niagara. But my recollection is that it was always very intermittent.

Even during the first hours of the raid I was immensely struck with everybody's calmness. The manager and his staff were splendid. Later on that night, in an underground air-raid shelter, a group of poor old ladies were a bit alarmed every now and then by the earthquake effects produced by the nearby dropping of the H.E. But visible alarm was strangely little in evidence anywhere that night around us. The real problem for everyone was where to go and what to do, and, later on, extreme tiredness. There was so little it seemed that we could do, and nowhere for many people to sit down when there was nothing for them to do. The fact was that we were all marooned in an island in the very centre of the terrific disturbance like a ship in the middle of a cyclone.

Ringed By Fire

When, about midnight, we had to leave the Victoria Hotel, we transferred to the Grosvenor Hotel across the road, where everybody was extraordinarily kind and the staff remarkably serene. By that time we were positively encircled by fire and smoke and water—but mostly by fire. As a spectacle it was magnificent in the extreme, and as the night wore on it got more and more magnificent. Most of us spent our time between the entrance hall of the hotel and its underground shelter.

For me, of course, the centre of everything was the Cathedral. I have always thought of Manchester Cathedral (and its attendant Chetham's Hospital) as a lovely jewel set in the midst of the most appalling and disgracefully unworthy surroundings. There must have been a period in its history when many of the citizens of Manchester had ceased to care what happened to the old church as long as they made a lot of money.

But that night the Cathedral in its setting was a thing of entrancing, shocking, devastating beauty. I choose these descriptive words advisedly. All around, instead of hideous ugliness, there were flames shooting, apparently, hundreds of feet into the sky.

Remember that the old Shambles was one vast bonfire, and the wind was driving in the direction of the Cathedral —wind so filled with sparks as to give the effect of golden rain. There was much more flame than smoke, so it seemed to me, and the roar of the flames was terrific. The stained-glass windows of the Cathedral were all lit up so as to produce a colour effect which was sublime. And there was " t'owd church," a fairy-like, scintillating thing in the midst of a blaze of fire.

Its surroundings looked for all the world like those horrific but fascinating pictures of the last days of Pompeii which we used to see in our childhood, and there was the

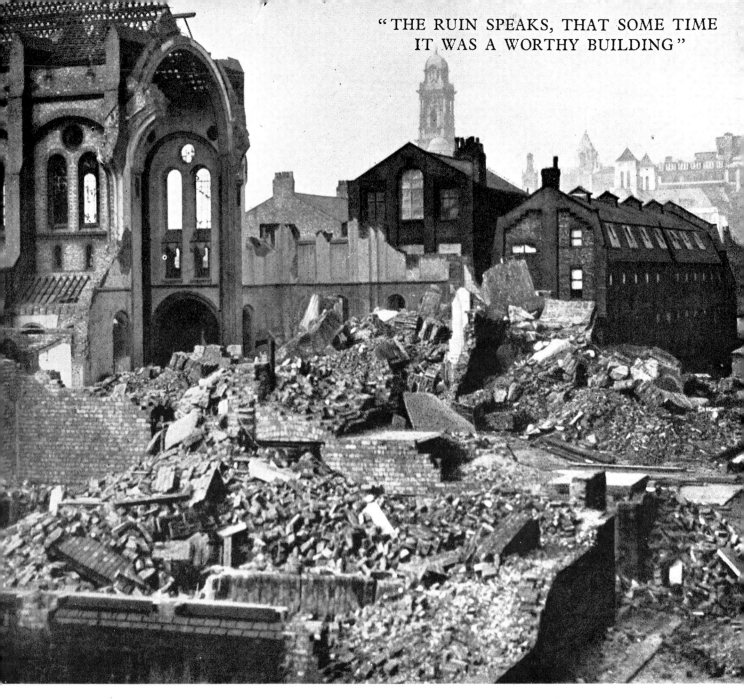

THE BATTERED REMAINS OF THE BEAUTIFUL ST. AUGUSTINE'S CHURCH, CHORLTON-ON-
MEDLOCK.   HERE ONE OF THE PRIESTS, FATHER STREET, WAS TRAPPED AND KILLED

old Cathedral, apparently unscathed and looking amazingly beautiful, right in the middle of it all. At 5 a.m. I was watching her from the door of the Grosvenor Hotel. I thought she was going victoriously to see it through ! I went down again into the shelter. I was very tired. I had not sat down for more than an hour all night.

At 6 a.m. or thereabouts the last bomb dropped—and it dropped on the north-east corner of the Cathedral. The noise of the fires was so terrific that we did not hear anything. The sensation was just like an earthquake—I had been in earthquakes before in India, so the sensation was not new.

With an officer in the Army pay department, after a little while, I went over to have a look. It was a sight indescribable. I am sorry we have no photograph of it

as it was then ; the excellent photographs of it in this volume were not, I think, allowed to be taken until after we had had nearly a week of clearing up.

The blast had lifted the whole lead roof of the Cathedral up and then dropped it back, miraculously, in place. Every window and door had gone ; chairs, ornaments, carpets, furnishings, had been just swept up into the air and dropped in heaps anywhere. The High Altar was just a heap of rubbish ten feet high. The two organs were scattered about in little bits. The great carved stalls were joined together in the centre so as to make an inverted V. The Lady Chapel, the Ely Chapel and much of the regimental chapel had simply disappeared. Showers of sparks still swept across the place, but the old Cathedral just refused to burn.

Manchester THE MANCHESTER REGIMENTAL CHAPEL, FORMERLY KNOWN AS THE DERBY CHAPEL.

VIEW FROM HIGH ALTAR, WITH HUMPHREY
CHETHAM MEMORIAL ON RIGHT **Cathedral**

And then it was that a tremendous thought gripped me—one that has never left me since.

This old place was the real Manchester, and I was actually glad she was battered about like this. How could she possibly have remained unscathed when so much else was destroyed? I did not want her to be saved as by a miracle—she must suffer with Manchester. She would never have been happy again if she had not suffered with the old city that had been built up around her, and which she and her predecessors on that site had watched over since long before the Norman Conquest.

Incidentally, the blast did not destroy the remains of the old Saxon church.

I began to feel hungry. Where could I get some food? Bishops, I knew, were " given to hospitality," and, anyway, I ought to tell the Bishop what had happened to his Cathedral, so I started to walk up Bury New Road. It was a long walk, for I had to find by-passes where fires blocked the road. I got to Bishopscourt at last, to find its chapel roof still smouldering—the Bishop, too, had had a night of it. We had a smoke, and then had some breakfast together. I remember I ate ravenously.

Then back I walked to the Cathedral. There I met my journalist friend; then the vergers and cleaners began to appear. I don't think they have ever recovered from the sight they saw then. Hubert Worthington, the Cathedral architect, came. He was a tower of strength. With unbelievable rapidity I was soon surrounded with a host of marvellous helpers. Old Mr. Brown, of Wilmslow, one of the greatest authorities on oak in the country, and a great lover of the Cathedral, turned up, saying that half a dozen of his best craftsmen were on the way. If the old oak stalls could be saved I knew they would save them. I think I was a bit fey.

Then I started thinking about my beloved Canon Peter Green. What had happened to him? Was he still in the land of the living? Nobody knew. So I walked over to St. Philip's, Salford. I found him positively exuberant after an all-night session similar to my own. He was like a man walking to the pavilion carrying his bat after knocking up a century.

Deanery a Shambles

Then I bethought me of my Deanery, and tried to cross the Ship Canal to reach it, via Stretford. It was an hour before I found a narrow bridge by which to cross it. All the roads were blocked. By the way, I have never succeeded in finding that bridge since. Eventually I reached the Deanery. It was a shambles. I found a corner of the dining-room sufficiently clear of dirt and rubbish to be able to change into clothes which I had succeeded in getting out of my windowless bedroom. I left the Deanery to go back to the Cathedral.

Outside I met Dr. Grieve, who was then Principal of the Lancashire Independent College. With tears in his eyes, he asked how bad was the damage to the Cathedral, and when I told him took a pound out of his pocket and insisted on me taking it. So it was a Congregational minister who gave the first donation for the rebuilding of Manchester Cathedral. Back I went.

It was only as I passed the Midland Hotel that I remembered that at 12-55 I had been due there to give a Christmas message to the Luncheon Club on the occasion of its annual children's lunch. I said to myself : " If any of them should by chance turn up, it would never do for you not to be there," so I dropped in. It was then 1-30, and they were just finishing their lunch. There were actually about seventy of them, as I remember, and going on with their programme as though nothing had happened !

That's Manchester !—it really is an amazing place ! And, the funny thing is that I had my address on me. I had written it three days before, and it was in my pocket-book. So, dirty and unshaved as I was, I gave my Christmas message and then went back to the Cathedral again.

" Better a Ruin——"

I think it was then that another conviction came to me—a conviction that has grown on me ever since. This old church you must leave a ruin unless Manchester itself WANTS to rebuild it ! Better a ruin as a memory of far-off days when she was " t'owd church " of Manchester than you should try to get Manchester to rebuild it against her real desire. Let us have reality in religion at all costs. As a ruin she speaks of a past when she really was the centre of all Manchester life.

If she is to rise from her ruins it must be because the Manchester of to-day still wants her to be the centre of its life, and itself rebuilds her as such. You must leave it to Manchester to decide. Manchester will rebuild her city. She will rebuild her shops and warehouses and cinemas ; she will rebuild her hospitals, and her schools ; she will make wide roads and open spaces, and bus stations and railway stations ; and let us hope she will build thousands of nice little homes for her citizens to dwell in.

But what will she feel about this old House of God ? Perhaps she will no longer want " t'owd church " except as a ruin. You must leave that to her to decide. Wherever, and however, she gets the money, no one but the real, authentic Manchester must rebuild " t'owd church." Anything else would be a sort of sacrilege. The old ruin would resent it in every stone and every oaken stall : the spirit of the place would cry out against it.

"I am t'owd church of Manchester," she cries. "You can, if you choose, make me more magnificent than ever I was. You have it in your power to put me in a setting that would show forth my beauty as never before in my history, which is your history, too. And how I should love it if you would.

"But let me remain a ruin in memory of your past rather than become the most magnificent Cathedral in the world with no real relation to your present or your future. Through the centuries that are past you grew up around me. I shall never be happy unless I remain central in your ever-growing life. Leave me as I am or else remake me, more beautiful than ever, as your very own, and even more your very own than ever before in our history. I would rather you should remain proud of me as a ruin than that you should let my rebuilding be the responsibility of others.

"I can only live by your love. If I have lost your love I would rather die, because my death would then be more to the glory of God than my life."

WORSHIPPERS AT THE CROSS STREET CHAPEL, HISTORIC HOME OF NONCONFORMITY IN THE CITY, HOLDING A MEMORIAL SERVICE IN THEIR ROOFLESS, BURNED-OUT BUILDING

A SAILOR AND HIS SWEETHEART HAD PLANNED TO WED AT ST. PETER'S, STRETFORD, BUT WHEN HIS LEAVE CAME THE CHURCH WAS SHATTERED. HERE THEY ARE SURVEYING THE RUINS AFTER THE CEREMONY IN THE NEARBY MISSION HALL

ALMOST EVERY HOUSE IN THIS ROW IN CATON STREET, HULME, HAD ITS FRONT RIPPED OFF BY BLAST FROM A HIGH-EXPLOSIVE BOMB WHICH FELL NEAR BY

IOO CHURCHES WERE DAMAGED

THE CATHEDRAL, of course, was not alone among the city's religious institutions to suffer at the hands of the raiders. There were other places of worship which held a hallowed place in the hearts of the people which virtually disappeared overnight.

Throughout the Manchester Diocese no fewer than eighty-six churches and mission churches, eighty-four church institutes and Sunday schools and close on fifty parsonage houses suffered at the hands of the raiders; every one of the seven places of worship belonging to the Manchester and Salford Mission had been damaged; twenty-seven Roman Catholic churches in the Salford Diocese, including the Salford Cathedral itself, sustained varying degrees of damage, as well as three convents in widely-separated parts of the area. The famous Cross Street Chapel, founded close on three centuries ago, was reduced to a mere shell.

The large hall of the Central Hall in Oldham Street, Manchester, which had resounded through the years to the fervour and eloquence of many famed preachers, was destroyed by fire and explosion; the equally-famous Albert Hall in Peter Street was saved from incendiaries only by the determination of amateur firefighters, after a hundred members of its congregation, their worship rudely interrupted by the enemy attack, had been shepherded into the safety of a nearby shelter.

Among the churches which were either completely destroyed or so badly damaged that repair was impossible were All Saints' Church which had stood as a landmark dominating Oxford Road, Manchester; its namesake, All Saints' at Stretford, which was completely demolished;

St. John's, Hulme, which was reduced to ruins together with its adjacent schools; and St. Peter's, Stretford, where a high-explosive bomb destroyed completely its impressive chancel and where, in a later attack, the church hall was burnt out.

Even the Bishop's Court and its private chapel did not emerge from the ordeal unscathed, and some ecclesiastical properties, such as the schools attached to the Stowell Memorial Church, Trafford Road, Salford, after sustaining damage in one attack, were repaired and then finally destroyed in a later attack.

Damage to church properties in the Manchester Diocese amounted to many hundreds of thousands of pounds. To that must be added the great value of Roman Catholic churches and those of other denominations which also suffered.

A Roman Catholic church in Manchester—St. Augustine's, Chorlton-on-Medlock—was the setting of a story of tragedy and heroism which could hardly be surpassed.

There were four priests at the church. Throughout a night of terror they fought the incendiary bombs which were showered on the district, helped to rescue people trapped in the wreckage of their homes, shepherded the residents to safety and gave absolution to the dying. Bombs of exceptionally heavy calibre fell on the church roof at a point where the choir transept joins the nave, wrecking the church, the clergy house and the church schools, and shattering dwellings around them.

Of those four priests one paid with his life, another was severely injured, and a third was slightly injured. The gaunt ruin of the church to-day stands as a grim monument to courage, devotion and sacrifice.

TWO YEARS OF RAIDS: A DIARY

ON JUNE 20, 1940, at a quarter-past three in the morning, the first alert was sounded in the Manchester area. Not a single 'plane was heard. There was no gunfire, yet it was, in a way, the most nerve-wracking experience the public was called upon to bear in the whole series of raids.

No one knew what to expect. The technique of cool but swift dressing, of laying one's things out before going to bed, had not been mastered. Husbands were too leisurely for their wives. Wives were too particular about their appearance to please their husbands. Children were often crotchety and resentful at being wakened from the untroubled sleep of childhood.

The little refinements of shelter comfort—the tea flask, the pillows and blankets, the bunks and easy chairs—had not been introduced. Even the order of precedence down the garden path to the shelter had not been established.

The alert lasted only thirty-three minutes, but in that time a new routine, which was to serve hundreds of thousands of people in good stead, had been learned. The veterans who heard the last and 329th alert over the area must have laughed at their early excitement and flurry.

The following record is, in effect, a diary of the raids on the Manchester area in which damage or casualties were reported. It does not pretend to be a bomb-by-bomb record, since many bombs fell on open ground, and caused neither casualties nor damage.

July 29, 1940.—Some H.E. fell in Salford. One damaged a transport time-keeping office at the corner of Trafford Road and Ordsall Lane. Others wrecked a railway truck in a storage yard in Ordsall Lane. Other H.E. bombs which fell close together damaged a portion of the boundary wall on land belonging to the English and Scottish Joint Co-operative Wholesale Society, Limited. Many house windows shattered.

August 8.—Enemy 'planes scattered copies of Hitler's "Last Appeal to Reason" over parts of Salford. No bombs. H.E. bomb shattered windows in Worsley.

August 28-29.—H.E. on Baguley and Brooklands, mostly in fields and gardens; no casualties. H.E. dropped at Worsley; some persons injured. H.E. caused fire at oil and petrol store, damaged scores of houses, and caused casualties at Altrincham.

August 29-30.—H.E. in Hulme and incendiaries in Moss Side, Alexandra Park, Rusholme and Platt Fields; house property damaged in Hulme and bomb on roof of Paulden's Store, Cavendish Street.

August 30-31.—Swinton and Pendlebury attacked. H.E. fell in Granville Street and Chorley Road, causing damage to houses and business premises.

August 31-September 1.—Raider which appeared to have followed railway lines from Knott Mill to Ardwick dropped H.E., several of which damaged commercial property, including a warehouse behind the Palace Theatre. This incident gave rise to a rumour that the Palace Theatre had been hit and many people killed. Another H.E. fell through the roof of the College of Technology, completely wrecking the Common Room and damaging two adjoining rooms. Two houses completely demolished in Lime Bank Street, Ardwick, by direct hit. A bomb fell through the railway bridge in Fairfield Street, leaving a clean hole.

September 3-4.—Chorlton-cum-Hardy district attacked. H.E. reported; houses in Hough End Avenue demolished. Gas main at junction of Nell Lane and Mauldeth Road West fractured.

September 4-5.—H.E. dropped in Weaste Cemetery; cemetery chapels damaged and many tombstones wrecked. House windows in Cemetery Road, Kirkham Street and Nelson Street shattered. Storage shed containing drums

FIRST HEAVY RAID—BY THE STANDARDS OF THOSE DAYS—WAS THE "BROADHEATH BLITZ," WHEN AN EARLY RAIDER HIT A SMALL, UNIMPORTANT FUEL TANK, WHICH ACTED AS A MAGNET TO THOSE WHO FOLLOWED

of highly-inflammable oil set on fire by H.E. at Messrs. Berry, Wiggins & Co., Ltd. depot, Eccles New Road, Weaste. Fire extinguished after three hours' fight by Salford Fire Brigade and A.F.S., assisted by units from other areas. Firemen were treated for burns at local hospitals.

Heavy bomb hit Old Peoples' Homes, Hope Hospital; one woman killed, three injured. Other H.E. in Pendleton area killed two people, seriously wounded 12 and caused slight injuries to others. Fireman, one warden and three First Aid Party personnel were among casualties. H.E. dropped on Worsley Golf Course, and two casualties caused at Swinton.

September 6-7.—H.E. dropped at Worsley and in pasture and potato fields at Irlam.

September 8-9.—H.E. on Didsbury and Northenden; stick of bombs fell on Withington Golf Course along the Mersey. No casualties.

September 9-10.—Casualties in incidents at Irlam, where H.E. were dropped. Liverpool road was blocked.

September 16.—String of H.E. fell across Heaton Park, fracturing a water service pipe at the hall. No casualties.

September 25-26.—Thirty-two sheep killed at Worsley, where H.E. were dropped. Incendiaries at Swinton and Stretford; no other casualties. H.E. fell at Sale, but there were neither casualties nor damage.

October 1-2.—Many H.E. and showers of incendiaries on Platt Fields, Moss Side, Fallowfield and Withington. Houses demolished in Walter Street, off Sherwood Street, Wilmslow Road, Fallowfield, and others damaged. Three dead, three injured in this incident. Four houses destroyed and many others damaged in Parkside Road, Moss Side. Occupiers were trapped in wreckage, and

FUTURE HOPES.—FIREMEN JOIN A TOAST DURING A BREAK ON CHRISTMAS MORNING

rescue work was long and difficult. Civil Defence messenger boy riding a cycle killed by bomb which fell in Wilmslow Road near White Lion Hotel; 12 other people seriously injured.

A new semi-detached house in Arnfield Road, Withington, wrecked. Family in Anderson shelter in garden escaped unhurt. Two people injured by bomb which fell opposite police station at Withington. In Moorfield Street, Withington, domestic surface shelter destroyed, and eight of the ten occupants killed; two others seriously injured.

Houses in Lower Kersal area of Salford were damaged and several fires started, but speedily extinguished by A.F.S. H.E. fell on Castle Irwell Racecourse; damage slight. Incendiary bombs fell on a jetty on the premises of Manchester Ship Canal Company close to an oil tanker discharging oil. They were promptly extinguished by ship's crew.

Fires caused at Trafford Park by incendiary bombs quickly put out; some houses damaged and others evacuated at Prestwich.

October 2-3.—H.E. fell in railway yard, Prince's Bridge, Water Street; two people slightly injured. Railway Company's stables damaged, but horses rescued. Houses were demolished in Grimshaw Lane, Newton Heath. Other H.E. in Church Lane and Holmfield Avenue West, Moston. Heavy bomb damaged cottage in grounds of large house at Parrs Wood.

Much more serious damage was reported from Salford, where bombs were dropped over a wide area. One H.E. fell in the grounds of Lancaster House, Vine Street, Kersal, the official residence of H.M. Judges of Assize. Firemen were fully occupied during the raid in dealing with a number of fires caused by oil bombs. A major fire developed when oil bombs penetrated the roof of a four-storey warehouse in Salford goods station, in which bales of cotton waste, rags and paper were stored. The building was gutted.

An H.E. fell through the roof of Salford Town Hall and tore down part of the exterior wall on East Market Street side, burying records of the Town Clerk's department and wrecking the Estate Office of the City Treasurer's department.

In the Marsden Street-Mountain Street area H.E. and a heavy oil incendiary demolished houses and damaged others, and started a serious fire. Three people were killed, two seriously injured, six slightly injured. A George Medal and a number of commendations were awarded personnel who rescued a woman and two children trapped in a bedroom in conditions of great danger and difficulty.

Casualties were caused at Prestwich, where oil bombs were dropped.

October 7-8.—Buildings and premises hit and damaged included city abattoirs and cleansing depot in Water Street, municipal flats at Hewart Road, Collyhurst, and a railway bridge in Gorton Street, Collyhurst. One person was killed and two were injured by an H.E. which fell on St. George's Tavern, Dawson Street, Hulme. In the flats two people were killed and there were other casualties.

Incendiaries fell in and near Victoria Station, but were put out without causing damage. There were fatal casualties also in Whalley Avenue, Brooks's Bar.

Bombs on Salford caused a number of minor fires in factories, houses and shops; several incendiaries on the

Town Hall were extinguished by members of the staff and A.F.S. personnel before they had done much damage. Large stocks of jam were damaged by water pumped on to a fierce fire at Mackie & Sons, Ltd., jam manufacturers, Irwell Street. The Duke of Lancaster Hotel, East Market Street, was badly damaged by fire.

At Stretford a long line of incendiaries was laid across the town from south to north, followed by several sticks of H.E. Most serious incidents were in Westwood Road, Essex Street, Old Trafford; Cornbrook Road, Old Trafford; and the Exhibition Inn, Stretford Road.

Some people were killed and injured in Trafford Park, and other casualties were caused at Urmston. An H.E. fell on the Golden Hill bowling green, Urmston. A stick of H.E. was dropped at Sale, but bombs fell in meadows by the River Mersey, without causing damage or casualties.

October 9.—Between 8-40 and 9-40 p.m. incendiaries were showered on areas in Chorlton-cum-Hardy, Moss Side and Chorlton-on-Medlock, and a stick of H.E. bombs, falling very close together in Zeta Street and Ashley Lane, Moston, destroyed several houses and killed one person and injured two others. Incendiary and H.E. bombs were also dropped in Swinton, Eccles, Urmston, Worsley and Trafford Park. Casualties included a member of a Rescue Party, who was killed.

October 10-11.—Three alerts during the hours of darkness. Two separate and distinct attacks developed over Chorlton, West Didsbury and Northenden. One person killed and two injured in Royle Green Road, Northenden, and identical casualties occurred in Hyde Street, Chorlton Road, Hulme, where an H.E. destroyed and damaged several houses. At East Didsbury, a house in Kingsway was destroyed, and a young woman was killed and two other people were injured.

An attack concentrated mainly on the Broughton district of Salford caused a considerable number of small fires, and a heavy bomb dropping on the footpath in Great Clowes Street caused severe blast damage to the Albert Park branch library. The building was afterwards demolished. About twenty people were sheltering in the public shelter in the basement of the library during the raid, and eight received minor injuries.

An oil incendiary demolished the blast wall of a surface shelter in Marshall Street, Salford, but only two of the many people in the shelter received injury. A fireman was injured in a fire in Broughton Lane.

H.E. on Dalton Street, Old Trafford, caused one death and a number of injuries, and people were temporarily evacuated from Dudley Street and Grafton Street, Old Trafford, following the discovery of an unexploded H.E.

October 11-12.—Districts principally involved were Moss Side, Hulme, Chorlton-on-Medlock, Rusholme, Fallowfield and Didsbury. Most serious incident was at Lincoln Street, Upper Moss Lane, Hulme, where seven people were killed and one was injured in the destruction of their homes. Three people were also killed in Carter Terrace, Denmark Road, Chorlton-on-Medlock.

RAID FORTUNE.—WITH HIS HOME TUMBLED DOWN RIGHT ON TOP OF THE ANDERSON SHELTER, HE ESCAPED UNHURT AND UNDISTURBED

CLEARANCE AREA. UNDER THE CITY'S PRE-WAR PLANS FOR BETTERING THE LIVING CONDITIONS OF ITS CITIZENS, SMALL BACK-TO-BACK HOUSES IN COLLYHURST, MANCHESTER, WERE PULLED DOWN TO MAKE WAY FOR IMPRESSIVE BLOCKS OF MODERN FLATS. BUT SOME OF THE HOMES IN THIS ONE MET THE FATE OF THEIR PREDECESSORS WHEN THE RAIDERS CAME.

TWO HUNDRED PEOPLE WERE IN AN UNDERGROUND
SHELTER AT THE OLD HULME TOWN HALL WHEN THIS
GAPING HOLE WAS TORN IN ITS SIDE BY A HEAVY-CALIBRE
BOMB THAT PARTLY DEMOLISHED THIS AND ADJOINING
BUILDINGS. THERE WERE RUMOURS OF A DISASTER, BUT
ALL THE SHELTERERS WERE ABLE TO LEAVE UNHARMED
THROUGH THE EMERGENCY EXITS

A heavy bomb penetrated two floors of the Manchester Royal Infirmary Nurses' Home, York Place, before exploding with devastating effect. All the personnel had taken shelter elsewhere, and no one was hurt. A delayed-action bomb fell in the University swimming bath at Burlington Street.

Other bombs fell in Baldock Road, East Didsbury; Wilmslow Road, near Cheadle Bridge; Tamworth Street, Hulme; Claremont Road, Rusholme; Raby Street, Moss Side; and Parrs Wood.

October 18-19.—H.E. dropped at Sale, causing damage to Worthington Street Council School and houses in Oulten Avenue, where four persons were injured. The slow line on the Altrincham to Manchester railway was blocked for a short time, and overhead electricity wires and telephones were damaged. The Home Office Approved School at Sale Moor was also damaged.

October 26.—H.E. on Cranmer Road and Sussex Avenue, Fog Lane, Didsbury; woman injured.

November 18.—Wythenshawe raided. In Moorcroft Road, off Button Lane, a corporation house received a direct hit, but the woman occupant escaped with minor injuries. A mother and four sons were injured in another house in Button Lane.

Houses were damaged in Derbyshire Avenue, near Sevenways, Stretford, and 12 people were treated for minor injuries and shock.

November 29-30.—Houses in Burnage and on Kingsway damaged by H.E., and there was slight damage to the

THE LANDLORD EXAMINES THE GAPING HOLE IN THE BOWLING GREEN ADJOINING THE NAG'S HEAD HOTEL AT DAVYHULME

Burnage High School for Boys. Windows in the shopping centre of Altrincham damaged by blast.

December 16.—A short, sharp raid on the Ancoats district. A stick of H.E. fell near the corner of Butler Street and Oldham Road, demolishing some shops and damaging 15 others. Two public houses were seriously damaged. Bombs were reported to be of light calibre, but with considerable blast effect. This raid occurred at 9 p.m., and the toll of life was correspondingly heavy. One of the killed was an A.R.P. warden who had been engaged conducting people to a shelter.

H.E. dropped at Stockport, causing three casualties, one of them fatal.

December 22-23 and 23-24.—The Blitz.

January 1-2, 1941.—Four people killed in shelter in Tealby Road, Gorton. A few minutes later a heavy bomb fell on a surface shelter in Burton Road, Withington, and nine people were killed, including several wardens. House property adjoining extensively damaged. Another heavy bomb fell in the garden of St. Paul's Rectory, Withington.

January 9-10.—H.E. and many incendiaries scattered widespread over the city. Several people injured by bomb which fell at junction of Victoria Avenue and Rochdale Road. A gas main was fractured and caught fire, and both roads were blocked for some time. Several houses demolished in Rushford Street, Longsight, where there were nine casualties, including one dead. Shelters in Mabfield Road, Withington, were damaged. Moseley Road Schools damaged by bomb which fell through roof.

Incendiaries and H.E. were dropped in Irlam, Prestwich, Worsley, Swinton, Urmston and Trafford Park. Three people were seriously and two slightly injured. Little damage.

February 4.—Two people injured at Stockport.

March 11.—A three-hours' raid in which H.E. fell in several districts of Manchester. Most serious incident in Victoria Street and Rutland Street, Hulme, where six people were killed by H.E. which destroyed several houses. Four people rescued alive from debris in the Erskine Street, Hulme, area. Stockport Road was blocked at several points by H.E. and unexploded bombs.

Two people killed, three injured, at Dartmouth Road, Chorlton-cum-Hardy, and one killed in a house in Torbay Road, Chorlton-cum-Hardy, from which four people, who had been trapped, were later rescued alive.

In Salford two serious fires were efficiently dealt with, although considerable damage was done. Ladywell Sanatorium, Hope Hospital and Eccles New Road flats were all hit in this raid.

Stretford, however, suffered more heavily than either Manchester or Salford. Most bombs fell in the neighbourhood of Trafford Wharf, Cornbrook Sidings and Pomona Docks. Enemy raiders set fire to a gas main in King's Road which, with the blaze from a laundry, acted as a beacon for later bombs. At one stage communications with the Trafford Park area were maintained only through the medium of a police radio motor car.

Damage in the Gorse Hill and Firswood areas was particularly severe, and St. Peter's School, Gorse Hill, and Clyne House Royal School for the Deaf were among a number of buildings partially destroyed by fire.

Damage to Manchester United Football Ground was later estimated at £50,000. The main centre stand was completely burned out, and dressing rooms and the medical room were destroyed. The club's equipment was lost, and there was damage to the covered stand on the popular side. Many incendiaries fell on the playing field.

H.E. caused damage in Partington Lane, Swinton, and there were casualties, one of them fatal.

April 15.—Incidents at Laundry Street, Littleton Road and Grecian Street, Salford, in which two people were killed and some injured.

May 1.—Confined to Chorlton-cum-Hardy. Most serious incident corner of Cavendish Road and Chatsworth Road, where some houses were demolished and others seriously damaged.

May 2-3.—House property in Chester Road, Wesley Street, Taylor's Road, Gorse Crescent, Moreton Avenue, Stanton Street, and Portland Road, Stretford, damaged by H.E. Number of people evacuated from Taylor's Road because of unexploded bomb. Four people were killed and four injured.

May 7-8.—Incidents in Darncombe Street, Moss Side; Meadow Street, Moss Side; and Whitchurch Road, Withington, accounted for most of the casualties.

H.E. bombs and incendiaries were reported in the Pendleton and Higher Broughton districts of Salford. Some casualties. Stretford authorities reported some killed and others injured in incidents in Skelton Road, Audley Avenue, and Moss Lane West.

At Eccles several people lost their lives or were injured. Many houses were damaged. A petrol store near Eccles Town Hall was set on fire by a direct hit. Several hours elapsed before the fire was brought under control. Half Edge Lane was blocked for several days by a heavy bomb, and two soldiers were killed by the same bomb. Two persons were injured at Sale when an H.E. dropped on the Mission Hall at Dargle Road and damaged adjoining property.

During the raid A.A. gunners had the terrific thrill of shooting down an enemy raider on the Torkington Golf Course on the Stockport-Hazel Grove boundary. The crew baled out and were quickly captured, two at Hazel Grove, one at Bramhall, and one at Cheadle.

June 1-2.—Next to the Blitz, the heaviest raid on the Manchester area. In Manchester H.E. and many incendiaries fell in a period of ninety minutes shortly after midnight on June 1, which was Whit Sunday. Destruction and loss of life was on a heavy scale.

Major fires and other outbreaks were dealt with by the fire service, nearly all in the city and Cheetham areas. Many people were rendered homeless, and a number of houses were demolished or damaged in varying degrees.

Rescue parties performed wonderful work in incidents at which their services were required. Heaviest damage was in Derby Street, Cheetham; Oldham Street; Southall Street, Strangeways; and at the Assize Courts. At all these points there were serious fires, and at the Jewish Hospital it became necessary, through fire, to evacuate a number of patients to Crumpsall Hospital.

Among other buildings damaged were the Gaiety Theatre, the Y.M.C.A., the College of Technology and

SOUVENIRS.—THE CIGARETTE-CARD AND STAMP COLLECTIONS SOON BECAME OUTMODED WHEN THE "SHRAPNEL" BEGAN TO RAIN DOWN

Manchester Police headquarters in South Street. Although the hit was close to a control centre, women on duty carried on their duties with great courage and calmness, and work was not interrupted. Two members of the Civil Defence Messenger Service were killed.

Salford was also heavily hit. Fourteen nurses were killed in the tragic incident at Salford Royal Hospital. Premises damaged included Threlfall's Brewery and Exchange Station.

Stretford had a number of casualties, and many houses were damaged. There were several fires, including one at the Public Hall; Longford Cinema was hit by incendiaries, but damage was slight. Several bombs fell in Swinton and Eccles, but there were no serious casualties.

October 25.—Heavy bombs dropped in the Broadheath district of Altrincham, killing some people and injuring others. Many houses were damaged as well as a railway station, shops and a school.

July 27, 1942.—Sneak raider flying just above the housetops dropped a stick of bombs in Palmerston Street, Hillkirk Street and Russell Street, Beswick, at breakfast-time. Three people were killed, seven were seriously injured and others were slightly injured. Five people who had been trapped in wreckage were rescued. More than 50 people were temporarily evacuated from the area owing to the presence of an unexploded bomb.

SEARCH

SOMEWHERE AMONG THIS RUBBLE LAY A BABY. IT WAS RESCUED AFTER SEVERAL HOURS BY THE MAN ON LEFT—UNHURT! IT HAD BEEN PROTECTED BY AN OVERTURNED CHAIR.

WOMEN HELPERS BRING ALONG HOT DRINKS FOR MEMBERS OF A RESCUE PARTY AFTER THEY HAD WORKED THROUGHOUT THE NIGHT.

WITH FACES DIRTY AND DRAWN FROM THEIR CEASELESS LABOURS, THE RESCUE MEN BRING AN INJURED WOMAN FROM HER WRECKED HOME.

FIREMEN HELP A MAN WHO HAD BEEN TRAPPED BUT ESCAPED UNINJURED, WHILE A WOMAN WARDEN WAITS WITH BLANKETS

THE WORK OF THE RESCUE SQUADS

LIKE EVERY OTHER branch of that amazingly comprehensive organisation which, from the adversity of war, has become Civil Defence as we know it to-day, the Rescue Service went into training long before the war began, believing it was acquiring skill which it would never be called upon to apply in practice. In fact, it was preparing for a task which man had seldom before been called upon to undertake, and when the history of this war on the home front comes to be written it will be found that those of the Rescue Service have etched some of its most vivid pages.

If you ask any of those who bore the brunt of rescue work in the air raids what has made the most indelible impression upon them they will tell you simply—the courage of people brought face to face with death, and particularly that of the children.

Sometimes it reveals itself with even a comic touch. There was, for instance, the eleven-year-old boy who had been buried under the ruins of his home. The rescue squad toiled long before they freed his head and shoulders. As they paused, one gruff rescuer wiped the grimy sweat from his brow, and muttered to a fellow worker: " By Jove, I could go a pint ! " The youngster overheard him. "Aye, and so could I," he innocently commented.

The first reaction of adults on being rescued is to inquire as to the safety of their loved ones, and then, once reassured, their anxiety is transferred to the homes in which their pride and their labours have been centred. One youngster, however, had more than a touch of fellow feeling. His little body bruised and broken, he sorrowfully surveyed the wreckage of his home from which the rescuers

had dragged him. "And ṭo think," he said, " my Dad only papered it last week."

In another part of the blitz-torn city a young brother and sister lay buried under bricks and wood and plaster. Gradually their heads and shoulders were freed—and then, with childish pride, in a cross-fire of patter, they began competing with each other as to who was the more seriously hurt. At length the pain which wracked them hushed their innocent chatter. A faint groan escaped the boy.

" What are you groaning about ? " his plucky little sister called across to him.

" It's all right you talking," he retorted, slightly impatiently. " You're older than I am."

When Viaduct Collapsed

In physical dimensions probably the greatest of the rescue workers' tasks followed the destruction of the railway viaduct at Egerton Street, Hulme. Supported by massive brick piers, the viaduct carried the railway line above a narrow peninsula of land, flanked, on the one side, by the River Medlock and, on the other, by the Bridgewater Canal, which drops by a series of locks underneath the shadow of the viaduct into the River Irwell. In the sunlight, grotesque ; in the gloom, ugly and forbidding.

During the blitz a bomb had penetrated one of the arches and inflicted serious damage to the viaduct, necessitating extensive repairs. Four of the arches later collapsed. Others were in immediate peril of collapsing. Ominous cracks appeared in the structure. Paper labels were pasted across the cracks and a workman, with flood-light focussed on the labels, was posted sentry, awaiting the first sign of the flimsy labels being torn asunder by the widening cracks.

But, without further warning, eight more of the arches collapsed like a pack of cards, burying a number of workmen and horses beneath great mounds of masonry. It is estimated that close on 2,000 tons of brickwork piled itself in that fantastic heap. The piers disintegrated into great blocks of brickwork, some weighing 40 tons and more. For days the rescue squads toiled against heavy odds until the bodies of the victims had been recovered.

In Withington a bomb dropped in a garden, tearing away the rear wall of a house and the corner of an Anderson shelter, which was left reposing on the lip of a great crater. A rescue worker on duty nearby hurried to the spot. "Anybody in ? " he cried out. " Yes," came the answer. "Are you all right ? " he asked. " Yes. But that was a close one. It must have been in the park across the road," came the bland comment from the shelter.

In Kingsway a dwelling house pancaked over a mother and her daughter. The younger woman was killed ; her mother was buried in the subsoil beneath the ruins of her home, and though nearly three hours elapsed before she could be rescued, she was not seriously wounded.

In the story of the rescue squads, the courage of rescued and rescuer is matched only by the ingenuity which had to be displayed. When a house in Englefield Road, Ryder Brow, Gorton, collapsed, trapping one young woman in the debris close by the blazing kitchen fire, the rescuers made a hole in the roof, wormed their way to her, and

PLAN OF ACTION.—SALFORD RESCUE SQUAD LEADERS CONFER TO DECIDE THEIR NEXT MOVE

held asbestos sheets between her and the fire until they could free her.

Long before the blitz the rescue squads had a grim foretaste of what was to be their lot. In one of the first raids on Manchester a high explosive bomb dropped in the neighbourhood of Yew Tree Avenue, Withington, blasting a motor car clean through the window into the bedroom of a house, and burying a young woman up to her armpits in debris.

When at last a rescuer fought his way to her through the bricks, plaster and timber, her sense of security was so great that she flung her arms round his leg, and would not let go. For two hours she clung fiercely to him while he struggled to get her free.

For tenacity, persistence and pluck there occurred a series of incidents during the raid of May, 1940, which can have few equals. A stick of four bombs dropped in Moss Side. One wrecked a house in Heywood Street. Cries for help led the search party to locate a woman trapped by debris in the cellar of her home. Water from a fractured water main was flooding the cellar and already was level with her waist.

Vainly the rescuers tried to divert the flow of water from the cellar. A pump was put to work, and two men clambered into the cellar through a small opening. The pump could not keep pace with the rising flood waters. A second pump was obtained and dropped through the opening—incidentally, cutting off the rescuers' chance of escape. With the two pumps holding the waters in check, they toiled for an hour and a half waist deep in water, and bending below water level to locate each piece of debris before they could free the woman. The woman weighed 18 stone, but she was rescued little the worse for her ordeal.

When a high explosive bomb wrecked the nurses' home at the Salford Royal Hospital, imprisoning nurses in the wreckage—twelve were killed outright and two others died later from their injuries—one rescue worker crawled through the wreckage to remain with one of the trapped nurses, talking to her and sustaining her courage. His colleagues worked for eleven hours, through the blast of another bomb which fell near by, showering them with rubble and masonry, before they rescued her, still alive.

Searched For Diamonds

Those are typical examples of the duties carried out by the rescue workers of Manchester, Salford, Stretford, Swinton, Sale, Altrincham and Eccles when they found themselves in the front line. They learnt to diagnose the nature of war damage so skilfully that they knew precisely how given types of buildings would collapse; they learnt to regard the fidelity of the domestic cat as a guide to where humans were awaiting aid.

And when the worst of the horrors were over they learnt how to salvage prized family possessions and furniture, to bring comfort to the victims, to retrieve valuables from blitzed safes, and riddle the ashes of the jeweller's stock to recover precious diamonds.

Heroes? They would not thank you for calling them that. They prefer to regard themselves as just plain citizens, doing their little bit to beat the enemy.

RAID FREAK.—NO ONE KNEW JUST HOW IT HAPPENED, BUT THIS CAR WAS FOUND IN A BEDROOM AFTER A BOMB HAD EXPLODED NEARBY

ORDEALS OF THE FIREFIGHTERS

I N THE STORY of the war in England there is no more honoured record than that of the firemen who fought the fires started by the Luftwaffe, and what was true of England in general was true in particular of the firemen who tackled the seemingly hopeless task of controlling the sea of fire which threatened to engulf Manchester and its neighbours throughout the fire blitz of December, 1940.

Professional firemen, in whom the nation had reposed its confidence in the days of peace, and amateur firemen, members of the then Auxiliary Fire Service, who had yet to face their real testing shared gloriously in the honour. From that crucible has emerged the National Fire Service of to-day, strong in the strength acquired in fiery ordeal, ready to face any test.

The enormity of the task which confronted them is told elsewhere in this book. Certainly no previous history of the industrial North could point to a parallel. And if honours were to be bestowed the local firemen, upon whom the major burden fell, would not grudge a share for other firemen who came to their assistance under the mutual aid scheme. These helpers came from bomb-shattered towns and cities and from peaceful, secluded villages to fight blazing buildings wherever they were needed.

The full story of their task will never be told. Every man lived his own grim drama ; nearly a score of them, including five who came to the city's aid from outside areas—all except one volunteer members of the old A.F.S.—carried their stories with them to the grave ; about eighty of them were injured.

" Amateurs " Took Command

At the height of the battle, " amateur " firemen—the term is not used disparagingly—and professional firemen of junior rank found themselves automatically taking command of sections to tackle fires which, in normal times, would have taxed the ingenuity and resourcefulness of high-ranking officers. One small section of men set out with a pump from Nell Lane, Withington, to tackle a blaze not far away. Before the night was out they had worked their way to the extreme side of Manchester—to Cheetham Hill Road—and had fought a dozen different fires in the process. They had man-handled their 10-cwt. pump all the way.

Though the toll on the men was heavy, there were countless providential escapes. When Exchange Station was blazing a group of firemen were training their jets against the face of the towering brick building. Suddenly a great colonnade of bricks collapsed outwards. The firemen turned about and ran to safety—all except one, who was working close to the base of the colonnade. Instead of following his colleagues, he darted inside the blazing station. His mates caught a glimpse of him as he disappeared into what looked like a furnace. A few minutes later he re-appeared, walking calmly up the station approach. His prompt and daring chance had saved his life.

Chance saved the lives of a complete section of men in another part of the city at the great conflagration which reduced Baxendale's warehouses to desolation and ruins. When the section arrived on the job they found two warehouses, separated by a street, on fire. The section leader held a hurried council of war, and they decided to toss a coin to determine which warehouse they should tackle first. The coin decided, and soon they had put out the fire in the first warehouse, and set about the second, a four-storey building in which the lift shaft was acting as a flue, sweeping the flames to every floor. The less experienced firemen were sent to the lower floors ; the more experienced tackled the upper floors.

On Demolished Turntable

A few minutes later there was a terrific explosion. Except for one man who was found reeling about in the building with a piece of metal piercing his neck, all the firemen escaped uninjured, apart from bruises. But when they regained the street they saw a gaping crater, and the warehouse in which they had first started to work had become a pile of rubble. A high-explosive of great calibre had dropped in the street immediately in front of the warehouse. The toss of the coin had saved their lives.

Their escape was equalled by another fireman who was directing a hosepipe from the head of an 85-foot turntable ladder on to a blazing building in St. Mary's Gate when the building was struck by a high-explosive bomb, blasting the walls asunder. The turntable, covered in debris and with a massive coping stone lodged across the centre of the chassis, was completely demolished, but the fireman's only injury was a broken toe !

Such episodes were typical, but they merely hint at the picture of the great struggle which faced the firemen. Fatigued almost beyond endurance by their efforts, sodden and frozen by the cascades of water streaming from doomed buildings or from the jets trained on them by their colleagues to enable them to keep at close grips with the flames which scorched them, they worked on.

Many of them were in action for thirty-six hours continuously before they could be relieved ; in the confusion of battle the feeding arrangements were not everywhere as perfect as they might have been, and city typists and shop girls cheerfully proffered their own parcels of sandwiches to sustain the firefighters. When at length many of them did return to the comfort of their stations and the hot food which awaited them they were too fatigued to eat, and slumped into deep sleep as they sat at their tables.

Their battle was over. And they had won—gloriously.

What were the reactions of the men themselves ? They were summed up this way later in the house journal of the Manchester A.F.S., " Stand-By " : We have a queer idea we ought still to be clinging, hour after hour, to jets, manhandling pumps, scrambling up and inside blazing buildings, dodging hot smoke and flames ; and, sounding about us all the time, the whining and crumping of bombs and the din of the gun barrage. *After such strain and excitement the present comparative inaction has an unreal quality*

DEFENDERS OF THE CITIES

THE FIRST WAVES of the enemy raiders were chugging their way across the tormented sky. The thunder of the guns rolled about the heavens. The gunners, silhouetted against the flashes, worked with demoniac energy, flinging up a curtain of splintering steel in defence of the Manchester area. Every gun counted ; every shot counted. There was speed, precision and smoothness as the men loaded and fired, loaded and fired.

In one of the batteries a gun temporarily ceased to fire. Part of the mechanism which swung the three-quarter-hundredweight shells into the breech had broken and become useless. Repair was impossible, but a strong man might, by sheer physical endurance, keep the gun in action. Yes, there was the man. One of the crew, not a Hercules, not a hero to his way of thinking—if he had given it any thought—but he kept the gun going. For five hours, without a break, refusing all relief, he pushed the huge shells by the strength of his good right arm up the tray into the breech.

At another site an incendiary fell on the huts in which the gunners were lodged. One by one the huts caught fire and blazed furiously, till the guns were almost ringed by flame. But the barrage did not stop, though the men knew that at any moment one of the Nazi 'planes might dive, as they often did, and spatter the site with machine-gun fire. More than one battery in the Manchester area was attacked in this way, for the look-outs several miles up in the dark sky were always on the watch for the tell-tale flashes of guns which might become too troublesome.

The anti-aircraft units of the Royal Artillery which defended the area on the two nights of the great attack were almost entirely from Liverpool and the West Country.

Only a few weeks earlier they had relieved the Manchester Territorial units which had previously manned the defences.

All were perfectly trained troops, who knew and loved their guns. They were so experienced that few of the idiosyncracies of the Luftwaffe pilots were unknown to them. They knew that some of them would fly through any barrage, heading straight for their target. They knew that others were not so bold, but would take evasive action at the first threat of danger ; would drop their bombs and turn for home.

Incidentally, this was the reason for so many bombs falling on the south side of the city. The barrage, which every week had been growing in intensity, was now strong enough to be an effective deterrent against accurate bombing. The first aim of the gunners was to destroy the enemy ; the second to prevent attacks being pressed home on the chosen targets.

Everybody knows what the main target was. If the Germans could have obliterated Trafford Park, or, at least, crippled its great industries, they would have seriously injured our war effort. The prize was worth winning, even at the price of heavy sacrifices, but it was denied them. Relatively few high-explosive or incendiary bombs fell on Trafford Park. The damage was negligible, and was soon repaired.

The work of the A.A. in the blitz was, therefore, of surpassing importance. Its reward was not spectacular in terms of 'planes brought down—anti-aircraft gunnery has advanced a lot since then—but any map of the Manchester area, pin-pointed with the bomb bursts of those two terrible nights, will show how very much more serious the damage might have been if the gunners had failed.

Many months before the outbreak of war the gun sites had been selected. They reached outwards more than ten miles into the surrounding country on all sides. The main armament consisted of four-point-fives and three-point-sevens, with various types of machine-guns for use against low-flying 'planes and flares. All were more than adequately supplied with ammunition. It was not the lack of shells which kept the guns silent at odd times in the blitz. The lulls occurred when the fighters were operating.

The nerve centre of the Manchester defence plan was a villa several miles from the centre of the city. Here was the operations room : here reports were received as the raiders flew over the coast : here the course of the raiders over the country was plotted. On the nights of December 22 and 23 the messages from Fighter Command showed the enemy to be approaching the city in two main streams, from the south and south-east, flying at between 12,000 and 17,000 feet, which was their usual altitude.

The guns on the south side of the city were thus the first to be engaged. Many of the raiders failed to penetrate the barrage, released their bombs, and turned away from the curtain of steel. Others bore north and came in from the north and west. The most daring pilots rode the storm, without flinching, straight to the target area. It was possible, on the information pouring into the operations room, to keep the batteries up-to-date with the track of the main formations across the sky.

Often there were two or three shells from a single gun in the air at the same time, directed at a point perhaps two miles in front of the attacking formations. If the air crews spotted the gun flashes in time, if they were not entirely indifferent to the desire for self-preservation, they had time to dive or turn, and so avoid the deadly rendezvous. It was a battle of wits, and of courage, with annihilation as the stake.

Every 'plane which found the target in the Battle of Manchester went through an inferno to get there. That, in a nutshell, was the achievement of the A.A. defenders. In nearly twenty hours of furious action hardly a 'plane crossed the roof of Manchester unchallenged. The losses and damage were grievous, but they might have been many times worse.

ACKNOWLEDGMENT

WITHOUT THE CO-OPERATION of regional and local authorities the compilation of a record so detailed and authentic as "Our Blitz" would have been impossible. The greater part of the story of the raids on the Greater Manchester area is here told for the first time ; it could not have been told without the facilities most freely placed at our disposal in the offices of authorities throughout the area.

For the privilege of access to files and for the encouragement and assistance given by chief officials and their staffs, "The Daily Dispatch" and "Evening Chronicle" offer their grateful thanks.

To the distinguished contributors to the book we tender thanks and appreciation.

All the photographs in this book were taken by staff photographers of "THE DAILY DISPATCH" and "EVENING CHRONICLE."

Requiescat in Pace

WE PLAN A FAIRER CITY

By the LORD MAYOR OF MANCHESTER
(Ald. Leonard B. Cox)

THE SPIRIT OF MANCHESTER, like that of other cities, towns and hamlets of this country, is one of unshakable determination to help in maintaining the country's war effort at its peak in order that victory be assured, "lest freedom should perish from the earth."

The frequent enemy air attacks on our city, which reached their peak with the ruthless and brutal raids of December, 1940, caused the loss of precious lives and the destruction of, or damage to, some of our noblest churches and other buildings, many of which enshrined the finest traditions of our public life. These losses only reaffirmed in the minds of the citizens the will to make further effort and sacrifice and to plan for the future a better way of life and a better city for themselves.

In this replanning we shall remember the high reputation that Manchester holds in the realms of freedom, art and culture. There is, however, much in our records which is unworthy of the city and its people. We see the mistakes, and we know that the coming of victory and peace will open a new chapter in world history, when we can start the task of rectifying past errors.

I picture our city looking to the future, working for modern ideals, and being influenced and guided by all that is best in her past history and traditions. This pre-supposes, among other things, a well-balanced and harmonious relationship between central and local government. However much the restricting powers of the central government may be justified in times of stress, such control should not be allowed to remain after the emergency has passed.

We recollect that local government was born before national government, that many of our national measures originated in local areas, and that, in fact, the mainspring of good government in this country lies in the initiative and vitality of the local bodies. With the return of peace Manchester hopes that the local authorities will have their former liberties not only restored but widened, so that they may each play their part in contributing to the welfare and reconstruction of the nation.

In this process of reconstruction education must be a vital element. Manchester looks to the new Education Bill with hopeful expectation, and sees in it the chance of a better education for all her young people. During enemy air raids some of our finest as well as some of our poorest schools were damaged or destroyed. We hope to rebuild in their places fine buildings where our young citizens may enjoy the advantages of modern, well-equipped colleges and schools, with ample playing fields and other facilities for healthy recreation.

The health services are receiving the city's attention, and much pioneer work has already been accomplished in the co-ordination of the voluntary and public medical services. Manchester envisages the time when medicine will be largely preventive and not merely curative, and when everyone in the community will be able to receive the best possible advice and attention.

The health of the people is closely related to housing. Enemy air attacks on Manchester destroyed much residential property, some of which was old and a disgrace to our city—a disgrace which we hope to wipe out by the building of new and better homes. Manchester is deeply concerned with this problem of housing. There can be no immediate improvement in health, or a satisfactory home-coming for the generation of young people fighting the enemy, unless there are houses in quantity and in quality. Manchester has, therefore, made plans for the complete elimination of slums, and aims at comfortable and well-planned homes for her citizens.

Enemy bombs have cleared several areas in the city, and some of these, we hope, will remain open spaces, so enabling it to be replanned with wide streets, dignified buildings, ample squares, green spaces and tree-bordered avenues. Brightness will be one of our keynotes, and we hope that our bomb-scarred railway stations will be modernised and made attractive, so that on arrival the traveller will gain a cheerful impression of the city.

We wish to advance in the spheres of art, music and drama. In the place of our world-famed Free Trade Hall, destroyed by enemy bombs—and from the platform of which so many great causes were launched—we wish to see arise a great palace of culture and enlightenment for the people; a home of music, drama and thought.

Manchester has for long been a centre of industry, and Manchester people confidently look to the future when their industries turn from war to peace production. They recognise that the transition will be difficult, and will call for new methods involving the use of the highest standards of industrial organisation, of business efficiency and of technical skill if the mills and factories are to render the maximum help in supplying the needs of an impoverished world and in restoring the productive and commercial activity of the nation.

We contemplate the time when the Manchester Ship Canal will be crowded with the ships of many nations, bearing products for the benefit of all, and when aeroplanes, no longer carriers of death and destruction, will transport passengers and merchandise to our airport from all parts of the world.

In short, Manchester aims to become the industrial, commercial and cultural capital of the North of England, populated by proud and happy citizens, well-informed and diligent.

These are the hopes and aspirations that we in Manchester cherish, confident that, with hard work and honest endeavour, we can achieve our ideals. Firm in the conviction of the righteousness of our country's cause and in the belief of our final victory, Manchester wills herself to rise, a new city, a noble monument to freedom and to the heroism of her citizens.

HOME FRONT, CHRISTMAS, 1940 —MILLER-ST., MANCHESTER

68

ASSIZE COURTS, ONE OF MANCHESTER'S FINEST GOTHIC BUILDINGS, DESTROYED BY FIRE IN THE WHIT WEEK RAID OF 1941